THRIFTY GOURMET'S
MEAT COOKBOOK

THRIFTY GOURMET'S MEAT COOKBOOK

BY

Ann Williams-Heller

A FAWCETT GOLD MEDAL BOOK
Fawcett Publications, Inc., Greenwich, Conn.

THRIFTY GOURMET'S MEAT COOKBOOK

May this book be thy friend and companion to "eat thy bread, and drink thy wine, and go thy way with a merry heart. . . ."

CONTENTS

3 LEFTOVERS WITH CHARACTER

THRIFTY GOURMET'S
MEAT COOKBOOK

1

THE STORY BEHIND THE RECIPES

What It's All About

This special thrift-meat cookbook has been written with you in mind. Its purpose is to bring more flavor and variety into your meals at less cost. Aware of your need and strong desire to spend less time in the kitchen, this book presents the new and easy cook-ahead way for thrift-meat preparation. This book is ready to be at your side every step of the way from planning to serving; and when you put it to work, it is as alive and useful as a friend. With any recipe you select, it tells what meat to look for, how much to buy, how to keep meat fresh before and after cooking, how to cook ahead and store or freeze, and how to serve planned or unplanned leftovers in ninety-nine different ways.

Beside the two hundred meat dishes from all corners of the world, there are thirty-five basic recipes for pot roasts, steaks, chops, burgers, and meat loaves; so, with the seasoning guide, you can create your own special dishes.

How to Use the Recipes

All the recipes use the thriftier meats available in self-service and other food markets. To make meat buying for a chosen recipe flexible, consult the illustrated meat choice list in each recipe section. Jot down a marketing list and shop with freedom and economy.

Most recipes give four to six servings. To divide in half, use one half of each ingredient. Use twice as much to double a recipe. Assemble all ingredients before you start to cook. Use level measurements.

All recipes list the approximate total preparation time and number of servings, and they suggest side dishes to round out the meal. Each cook-ahead dish has a star (★) next to its title. Some recipes look long because they give every step for foolproof preparation so that the inexperienced cook, too, can follow with success and ease.

Meet the Meats

Meat is our favorite fare. American meals are planned around meat. There is more to that tender morsel of meat than good taste; it supplies good proteins together with B-vitamins, phosphorus, iron, and energy. Protein (from the Greek for "I am first") maintains the very life of your body cells. From top to toe you are protein and you need protein in your daily meals. Remember "I am first" when you plan your main-dish meat.

Meat is our most expensive single food. However, even with today's skyrocketing prices, you can stretch food dollars with the less tender cuts of meat. They are as nutritious as the more tender, higher-priced cuts and are often more flavorful and juicy. Thrifty, less tender meats are in plentiful supply; unfortunately many homemakers do not know how to prepare them properly.

In other lands, however, they are cooked with imagination and love. Hungarian gulyas, German sauerbraten, Italian osso buco, Austrian boiled beef, Irish stew—all are great dishes made with the less tender cuts; recipes for these dishes are found in these pages.

Available Variety

There is a flavorful meat for every purse, taste, and occasion; enough variety to serve a different meat every day of the year. You can choose from beef, lamb, pork, or veal, or from the variety meats (brains, heart, kidneys, liver, sweetbreads, tongue, and tripe). Beef is America's favorite; in some regions there is a traditional preference for pork or other meats. Meat comes to market fresh and prepackaged fresh, quick-frozen, cured, smoked, canned, and dried, as well as in an ever-growing line of ready-to-serve meats.

How to Know Meat Quality

To guide your shopping, a quality description of beef, lamb, pork, and veal precedes each recipe section.

The meat you buy is protected by our government. The inspection stamp "U.S. Inspected and Passed" guarantees that, under sanitary conditions, healthy animals have been slaughtered and their meat processed so that it is entirely suitable for consumption. About 80 percent of all commercially sold meat is federally inspected and a large part of the remaining 20 percent is under state or city inspection.

There are two kinds of government grading stamps or marks on the wholesale meat carcass. One is for "Conformation, Finish, and Quality" according to official standard specifications; the other, for "Purity and Wholesomeness" is required by law on all meat sold in interstate commerce.

The first three quality grades for retail beef, lamb, and veal are: U.S. Prime, U.S. Choice, and U.S. Good. The fourth grade for beef and veal is U.S. Standard, and for lamb it is U.S. Utility. Although there are federal grades for pork, they have not been widely used. Many cuts of pork, especially those which have been cured or smoked, carry the packer's brand identification.

If you should need more detailed information write to: Meat Grading Branch, Live Stock Division, Consumer and Marketing Service, U.S. Department of Agriculture, Washington, D.C. 20250.

Many meat packers and retailers establish their own grade names, known as *brand names,* to identify their products. Some brands may parallel the government grades. Each company will give information concerning its own brand names upon request.

How to Select Meat

In self-service markets, meat is labeled with the name of the cut, its grade, price per pound, and total cost. If you know what you want, selection is simple. In markets where meat is not packaged, tell the meatman what you want to cook, and he will select the cut you need.

Use the illustrated meat descriptions at the beginning of each recipe section, so that you can recognize the different cuts suitable for a recipe. With experience you will learn to identify meat cuts by shape, color, and appearance rather than by labels, and will feel confident about making substitutions when you find a "special" at the meat counter. Identification is simpler when the cut has a part of the bone; when there is no bone or when it has been removed, the shape is a clue. Names of cuts vary around the country, which is confusing to the traveling homemaker. For more about meat, its flesh, bones, and fat, see *Meat Composition*.

How Much Meat to Buy

The amount of bone and fat determines the number of servings in a pound of meat. Here is a simple yardstick:

KIND OF MEAT	APPROXIMATE SERVINGS PER POUND
Boneless or lean ground	3–4
With medium amount of bone (as chops, steaks)	2–3
With large amount of bone (as shortribs, spareribs)	2–1

Since the appetites of family and guests vary, it is difficult to estimate "average" servings accurately. The kind and quantity of side dishes affect the amount of meat eaten. For festive occasions and outdoor meals, larger meat servings are indicated.

How to Figure Meat Costs

Thrifty homemakers figure meat in cost per serving. Find it by dividing total cost by the number of servings the meat will yield. If a two-pound piece costs $3.00 and yields three servings per pound you have six servings at a cost of 50 cents per serving.

How to Cook Meat

Regardless of kind and quality grade, all meat divides naturally into two groups: (1) the tender (higher priced) cuts; and (2) the less tender (more thrifty) cuts, which are made tender by slow cooking with added liquid or by other means.

Accordingly, there are *two basic ways* of cooking meat. (1) All tender cuts and ground meat should be cooked by *dry heat* or open cooking: oven-roasting or baking, broiling or pan-broiling, cooking on spit or open fire, also sautéing or pan-frying in very little fat. All meat cooked by dry heat (except pork and veal) can be served in varying degrees of doneness: rare, medium, or well done. (2) All less tender cuts must be cooked by *moist heat* tightly covered: braising or simmering at very low temperature in just enough liquid to let the locked-in steam soften the meat's fibers and also unlock its delicate flavor. All meat cooked by moist heat (and all pork and veal cooked by dry heat) must be served well done and fork tender. When in doubt about a meat cut's tenderness, braise instead of baking or broiling.

Seven Ways to Spend Less Time in the Kitchen

Thrifty meat cooking is easy. It may also be time-saving. Braised meats (more than half this book's recipes) require much less of your time in the kitchen than you believe. It is not the actual braising time that counts but rather how much of your time is needed to get a meat dish ready for the table. While a pot roast takes two to four hours, your time in the kitchen is only fifteen minutes at the start, a minute's checking every hour or so, and ten or fifteen minutes to get the meat table-ready.

To spend less time in the kitchen.

1. *Cook ahead.* Braised meat is cook-ahead food. Reheating improves its flavor. Cook tomorrow's meat tonight; tomorrow, dinner will be ready in one half-hour. (Calorie-watchers: Braised meats can be made almost fat-free by lifting solidified fat from refrigerated meat and juices.)

2. *Use a timer for pot-watching.* An inexpensive timer from the houseware store lets you leave the kitchen with a free mind. With the timer set and by your side, evening hours are perfect for cooking ahead. After browning a pot roast or stew, set the timer for one hour and take it with you. When it rings, return to the kitchen for a minute or two. Then set the timer for your next pot-watching.

3. *Serve plan-over meals.* Unless you serve a large family or guests, a larger piece of meat—pot roast, boiled beef, ham—will give you cooked meat for two or three more meals. When you shop and cook only once with leftovers in mind, you cut your kitchen time in the days ahead to about one half-hour. See *Leftovers with Character.*

4. *Double-batch.* Cook twice the quantity of a recipe and freeze one half for future use. This saves time—and money, too, especially if you watch for midweek specials advertised in local papers, on TV and radio, and in food markets. (But remember that a bargain is only a bargain if you can use it.)

5. *Pressure-cook.* A large pressure-cooker will cook a good-sized pot roast or so-called boiled meat in one third to one half its usual cooking time. Use your timer to avoid overcooking.

6. *Use kitchen shortcuts.* Save precious minutes and

steps by using the forty-four easy-to-remember tricks and hints on page 251.

7. *Use the Index.* Let the index at the back of this book be your fact-finder for all you want to know as you plan your shopping, refrigerate, thaw or not thaw, cook, or chop an onion without tears.

Seven Ways to Cook the Thriftier Cuts

Proper cooking improves and develops flavor, tenderness, juiciness, and palatability of meat. For best results, always cook a cut of meat according to the method best suited for it. Below are the seven basic ways to cook less costly meats. For step-by-step directions on cooking any particular cut, see the Index for the Basic Recipe under pot roasts, steaks, stews, baked or broiled ham, etc.

1. *Braising* for pot roasts, steaks, and stewlike dishes.

2. *Simmering* for large meat cuts, such as fresh beef brisket, corned beef, soup meat, smoked tongue or pork, and "boiled" dinners.

3. *Broiling or Grilling* for tender or tenderized steaks and chops, one to two inches thick; also for ground-meat patties and some variety meats.

4. *Pan-Broiling or Griddle-Broiling* for steaks, chops, and ground patties up to one inch thick.

5. *Pan-Frying (Sautéing)* for thin steaks and chops, patties, breaded or floured sliced meat, also small frozen cuts, such as sliced liver and meat patties.

6. *Roasting (Baking)* for large tender cuts of lamb, pork, veal, ham, and meat loaves.

7. *Pressure-Cooking* for pot roasts, "boiled" meat, braised steaks, and stews.

Seven Ways to Make Meat Tender

Here are simple ways to soften the fibers of less tender cuts of meat.

Before Braising

1. For large cuts: Marinate meat overnight or longer as recipe directs. Put meat in a large utensil. Add a marinade containing vinegar or wine, or both. Cover and refrigerate. Turn and baste occasionally. Save marinade for further use.

During Braising

2. For cubed meat, steaks, chops, and pot roasts: Add tenderizing liquids in small quantity to braising liquid. Tenderizing liquids are wine, beer, tomato juice, ginger ale, soy sauce, canned pineapple juice, and cranberry sauce. Use as the liquid fits the taste of the dish.

3. For steaks and chops no thicker than 1 to 1¼ inches: Add tenderizing liquid as above.

Before Broiling

4. For kabobs: Marinate meat as above. Use marinade for basting, especially when cooking outdoors.

5. For larger steaks and chops: Sprinkle with an enzymatic, commercial, powdered instant meat tenderizer, available seasoned and unseasoned. Follow the manufacturer's directions. Watch reduced broiling time.

6. For thin steaks and chops: At least thirty minutes before cooking, work a few drops of olive oil into meat with your fingertips—or

7. Pound or beat the meat with a mallet, cleaver, or rolling pin.

Meat Storage in Transit

All meat is perishable, whether fresh, cooked, processed, or frozen. Avoid waste and keep meat safe to eat by keeping it in the cold. Unless you cook it immediately, refrigerate meat at once for use within a few days. Freeze it for later use. Place commercially frozen meat in the freezer at once. And remember: Whatever you do, it is a temporary storage. See *Storage Time for Fresh, Processed, and Home-Cooked Meat* and use meat before maximum time indicated.

How to Refrigerate Properly

Fresh meat: As soon as possible after purchase, store in the special meat keeper or in the coldest non-freezing part of your refrigerator (36° F. to 40° F.).

Remove store wrapper. Wrap loosely in waxed paper or foil, or leave unwrapped since partial drying out of the meat's surface increases its keeping quality. Prepackaged meat, if used within a day, can be stored in its original self-service wrapper; if stored for more than one day, loosen wrapping at the ends to allow for air circulation. Precook brains and sweetbreads instantly; also tripe if it has not already been cooked when purchased. Store ground meat for no longer than one day: it loses its flavor easily. Leave processed meats (cured, smoked, sausages, and ready-to-serve) in their original wrappings.

Home-cooked meat: Chill rapidly for one half hour or less. Cover container(s) tightly. Refrigerate in the coldest non-freezing part of the refrigerator. Never leave cooked meat outside the refrigerator for more than two hours.

Pot Roasts: Place meat, vegetables, and meat juices in separate containers.

Stews: Put in one container.

To speed-cool: Place uncovered container in a pan of cold water with plenty of ice cubes. Change water occasionally; add ice cubes as needed.

How to Store in Home Freezer

Before you prepare meat for freezing, consult your freezer instruction book. All meat must be in top condition for freezing and kept hard-frozen until ready to use.

For already-frozen meat, the freezer temperature should be 0°F. or lower. For the actual freezing of fresh or cooked meat, it should be *minus* 10°F. to *minus* 25°F. Allow space for air circulation between the packages of fresh or cooked meat while freezing; and if possible, have them touch the freezer's wall for speedier freezing. Use the refrigerator's frozen food storage compartment or ice cube section for freezing *only* if it is in a separate section and has a separate door and a temperature of 0°F. or less.

How to Prepare Meat for Freezing

Fresh meat: Trim excess fat from roasts, steaks, and chops. Remove bones when practical to conserve freezer space. Wrap in "family-size" packages whenever possible. Pack stew meat in recipe amounts or quantities convenient to serve. Shape unseasoned ground meat into patties; to facilitate future separation and speedier thawing, place double thickness of waxed paper or freezer-wrap between individual packages. Make flat packages; they store better than rolls or folds.

Freeze-wrap meat tightly in a moisture- and vapor-proof sheet wrapping (aluminum freezer foil or plastic wrap) or place in a plastic freezer bag. Press out as much air as possible before sealing with freezer tape. Label and date all packages properly; it is often helpful to indicate weight and approximate number of servings on larger cuts.

Home-cooked meat: Cook until firm-tender; avoid overcooking for freezing. Cool hot meat quickly as for refrigerator storage. Slice meat loaves in serving portions. Remove fat from meat, and potatoes from stews and pot roasts.

Freeze roasts, gravy, and vegetables in separate containers. Freeze stews "as is," and remove any potatoes, since they do not freeze well. Do NOT freeze broiled or fried meat.

Freeze-wrap cooked meat tightly in paper that is moisture- and vapor-proof, paper freezer bags, plastic jars or straight-sided containers made of clear plastic or aluminum foil. Seal with freezer tape. Label and date all packages properly.

STORAGE TIME FOR FRESH, PROCESSED, AND HOME-COOKED MEAT

(To maintain quality)

FRESH MEAT	Refrigerator 36° F. to 40° F. DAYS	Freezer 0° F. or less MONTHS
Beef	2–4	6–12
Lamb	2–4	6–9
Pork	2–4	3–6
Veal	2–4	6–9
Ground		
beef	1–2	3–4
lamb	1–2	3–4
pork	1–2	1–3
veal	1–2	3–4
Stew meats	1–2	2–3
Variety meats	1–2	3–4
Sausage (pork)	1 week	2
PROCESSED MEAT		
Cured/Smoked		
bacon	5–7	1
beef, corned	1 week	2 weeks
frankfurters	4–5	1
ham, whole*	1 week	2
ham slices	3–4	2
sausage (smoked)	3–7)	
sausage (dry and semidry)	14–21)	freezing not
Luncheon meats	1 week)	recommended
COOKED MEAT		
Roasts and larger cuts of unsliced meat	3–5	2–3
Stews and Swiss steak	3–4	2–3
Hams and picnics	7	1–2

*Unopened canned ham will keep in the refrigerator up to 1 year. If not labeled "perishable" or "keep in refrigerator," it is stored on the pantry shelf.

To Thaw or Not to Thaw?

While most frozen meat may be cooked or reheated without previous thawing, it is better to defrost larger pieces of frozen meat before cooking until you are experienced. Even though freezing softens the fiber, frozen meat still takes about 1⅓ to 1½ times longer to be table-ready than fresh or thawed meat does.

Cook before Thawing

Frozen meat patties and sliced meat loaves are easy to broil or pan-broil; so are thin steaks and chops. Thick frozen steaks and chops must be broiled farther from the heat than defrosted ones, so that the meat will be cooked to desired doneness without charring on the outside.

Proceed as with fresh meat; turn often with slotted pancake turner and season as you cook.

Cooked combination dishes, such as stews, should always be heated without previous thawing. Place frozen food in a casserole or shallow pan and heat in a moderate (350° F.) oven; or heat in top of double boiler over hot water.

Cook after Thawing

Always cook thawed meat promptly while still cold. The cooking time of thawed uncooked meat may be slightly shorter than for fresh meat. Already cooked meat needs reheating only.

How to Thaw Frozen Meat

Leave frozen meat in freezer wrap. Depending on your time, use one of these three ways to thaw safely:

1. *In the refrigerator,* thaw for about 3 to 5 hours per pound of meat; about 4 to 7 hours per pound for larger cuts; about 12 to 14 hours per pound for 1-inch-thick steaks.

2. *At room temperature,* thaw for about 1 to 2 hours per pound of meat; about 2 to 3 hours per pound for larger cuts; about 2 to 4 hours per pound for 1-inch-thick steaks. If possible, place meat in front of an electric fan. Actual defrosting time depends also on the temperature in the room.

3. *Under running water,* thaw either directly under the faucet or in a water-filled pan. The water must be cold, never warm or hot. This method is primarily recommended for meats that are to be simmered or braised. Even then, it is wise to put the freeze-wrapped meat in a well-tied plastic bag.

For all commercially frozen meat, follow package directions.

Can Thawed Meat Be Refrozen? You may refreeze thawed uncooked meat only after it has been completely cooked. Do NOT refreeze cooked meat that has been thawed and reheated.

And remember: *Freezing Weakens Spices.* After reheating frozen cooked meat dishes and before serving, check and correct the seasoning.

2

THE RECIPES

BEEF

The flesh of good-quality fresh beef is bright cherry red, firm, fine in grain and well streaked with marbled fat. The exterior fat is creamy white and brittle. The bones of young beef are porous and red. In lower grades the red of the lean deepens and the fat is yellowish.

BEEF POT ROASTS

Whenever possible, cook ahead (at least one day before serving) and plan on leftovers.

How to Plan Pot Roast Servings

ONE AVERAGE SERVING	POUNDS PER SERVING
Bone-in meat	⅓–½
Boneless meat	¼

For step-by-step directions on how to refrigerate and freeze fresh and cooked pot roast, see *Meat Storage in Transit*. See also *Carving Made Easy*.

19

Cuts to Select for Beef Pot Roasts

Blade chuck roast: with blade bone and some fat; sometimes available boned.

Blade (chuck) pot roast

Arm (or round bone) chuck roast: with small round bone and some fat.

Arm (chuck) pot roast

Heel of round: a wedge-shaped boneless cut.

Heel of round

English or Boston roast: a rectangular, boneless cut with two or three ribs; with alternating layers of lean and fat; sometimes available boned.

English or Boston cut

Boneless chuck roast: a meaty cut with little marbling.

Boneless chuck roast

Boneless rolled chuck roast: a tied compact roast; no outer layer of fat.

Boneless rolled chuck roast

Rolled plate roast: a rolled and tied compact roast; moderate amount of fat.

Rolled plate

"Baby pot roasts" (crosscut beef shanks and *short ribs):* for small-family or individual servings; both cuts with some bones and fat.

Crosscut shanks

Short ribs

WHEN ON "SPECIAL SALE":

Rump roast: a triangular cut with portion of rump and tail bone; moderate amount of fat.

Rump roast

Rolled rump roast: boneless meat tied in a compact roast; usually covered with a thin layer of fat.

Rolled rump roast

Sirloin tip roast: a triangular meaty cut; best buy is boned, rolled, and tied.

Sirloin tip

The Basic Beef Pot Roast ★

Total Time:
2½–3½ hours for bone-in meat,
3–4 hours for boneless meat
Serves:
  bone-in meat, 6 or more
  boneless meat, 8 or more

  3- to 4-pound beef pot roast
  2 to 3 tablespoons fat
  1 teaspoon salt (more or less to taste)
  ½ teaspoon (or less) black pepper
  ½ cup chopped onions (more or less to taste)
  ½ to ¾ cup beef bouillon, wine or water

1. Select cooking utensil with tight-fitting cover. See *Pots and Pans*.

2. In hot fat, brown meat well on all sides, about 15 minutes, to seal in meat juices. Turn with tongs or pancake turner. After browning, pour off excess fat, if necessary.

3. Season meat with salt and pepper or any seasoning to taste. See *Flavors to Flatter*.

4. Start braising. Add onions and brown for a few minutes; stir occasionally. Add liquid. Cover cooker tightly. Braise over very low heat on top of stove or in a slow (325° F.) oven, an electric table cooker or a pressure cooker. Note the time. Set your portable timer for about 1 hour later; take it with you when you leave the kitchen. Turn and baste meat about once every hour. If needed at such time, add hot liquid in small quantities.

5. *If the meat is to be served immediately after cooking,* braise until "fork-tender," that is, well done when pierced with a fork. Do not overcook. Braising time will be from 2½ to 3½ hours, depending on the cut of meat, its quality

and thickness, and its amount of bone and fat. In pressure cooking, figure about one-half of total braising time after browning as you follow manufacturer's directions.

Remove meat to hot platter; keep hot. Rest meat for 15 minutes before slicing. Skim excess fat from meat juices, if necessary, and reserve for gravy. See time-saving hint on page 252.

To serve: Reheat sliced pot roast in meat juices or gravy if necessary. Make gravy as below (step 7). Serve gravy in separate dish.

6. *If meat is cooked ahead:* Braise only until "firm—tender," that is, some 15 to 25 minutes less than total cooking time, since the meat will simmer again when reheated.

Cool and refrigerate meat and meat juices immediately after braising; follow step-by-step directions on page 11.

To serve: About 45 minutes before serving, remove refrigerated meat and meat juices. Lift fat from meat juices; reserve about 3 tablespoons fat if you want to make a thick gravy. Cut thin, even slices off meat as needed; allow for extra helpings. Refrigerate remaining meat instantly, as before.

One-half hour before serving, heat meat juices slowly in covered heavy skillet on top of stove. Check seasoning; add herbs and spices to taste; see *Flavors to Flatter.*

NOTE: If, in a recipe, ingredients such as sour cream or canned vegetables are to be added shortly before serving, always add to meat juices that have been well heated.

Make gravy as below (step 7), if desired. Add sliced meat. Cover and simmer over very low heat until thoroughly heated. Serve as above.

7. *To make gravy:* Heat 3 tablespoons meat fat in cooker. Measure meat juices; add enough water or bouillon to make 2 cups. Mix 2 to 3 tablespoons flour with ¼ cup cold water to a smooth paste; stir into hot meat juices. Simmer until thickened, stirring constantly. Season to taste with additional salt and pepper or any other seasoning.

Serve with any green or yellow vegetable; potatoes or

rice; noodles, spaghetti or other pasta; and a tossed green salad or cole slaw. Garnish. See *Eatable Garnishes*.

Curried Pot Roast of Beef ★

About 45 minutes before meat is tender, mix 2 tablespoons curry powder and 1 teaspoon sugar with ½ cup beef or chicken bouillon. Stir into meat juices of the Basic Beef Pot Roast and add 4 scraped medium-sized carrots, 8 peeled small potatoes, 8 peeled small white onions; or ½ pound each of whole green (snap) beans and mushrooms. Finish cooking as above.

Barbecued Beef Pot Roast ★

Instead of bouillon in the Basic Beef Pot Roast, add 2 tablespoons Worcestershire sauce, 1 cup chili sauce or catsup, 1 teaspoon sugar and ¼ teaspoon dry mustard blended with ½ cup hot water or wine. Finish cooking as before.

Chili Pot Roast of Beef ★

About 1 hour before meat is tender, add 2 cups cooked or canned tomatoes blended with 1 teaspoon chili powder and ½ teaspoon prepared mustard to the Basic Beef Pot Roast. Finish cooking as above.

German Sauerbraten with Spätzle ★
(Marinated Pot Roast with Mini-Dumplings)

Marinate at least 2 days; if possible, 3 days.

Total Time: Serves: 8 or more
to marinate, 2–3 days
to prepare, about 3 hours

    3- to 4-pound beef pot roast, boneless chuck, or heel of round

Marinade:
- ½ tablespoon salt
- ½ teaspoon black pepper
- ½ teaspoon paprika
- 2 large onions, cut up
- 2 large carrots, scraped and quartered
- 1 large celery stalk, cut up
- 1 lemon, sliced
- 6 whole cloves
- 6 (or more) peppercorns
- 2 bay leaves
- 2 cups (or more) cider or wine vinegar

- 4 tablespoons butter or margarine
- ½ cup seedless raisins
- 2 tablespoons sugar
- ¾ cup coarse gingersnap crumbs
- Spätzle recipe

To marinate: Place meat in earthenware, glass, or enamel bowl; add marinade and enough vinegar to cover meat. Cover bowl; refrigerate for at least 2 days. Once a day, turn meat with a wooden spoon and baste with liquid in bowl.

To cook: Drain meat; strain marinade and reserve. In Dutch oven or large heavy skillet, heat 2 tablespoons butter; brown meat slowly on all sides, about 15 minutes. Add 2 cups marinade and raisins; bring to quick boil. Cover tightly. Braise over very low heat until meat is fork-tender, about 2½ hours. Turn meat once every hour and baste. If necessary, add more marinade. When tender, remove meat to hot platter; keep hot. Let meat rest for 15 minutes.

To make gravy: Skim fat off meat juices if necessary; add marinade or water to make 1½ cups. Add the remaining 2 tablespoons butter, sugar, and gingersnaps to meat juices; stir until gravy is smooth; remove from heat. *NOTE:* For a thicker gravy, blend 2 tablespoons flour into ¼ cup meat juices and mix with gingersnaps before making the gravy.

To serve: Slice meat before serving or at the table. Spoon part of gravy over meat; serve remaining gravy in separate dish. Serve with Spätzle or buttered noodles.

Spätzle (Mini-Dumplings)

Total Time: about 25 minutes   Serves: 6 or more

    2 cups flour
    2 eggs, slightly beaten
    ½ teaspoon salt
    2 tablespoons cold water

Sift flour into a bowl; make a well in the center; add ingredients in order given; knead with hands until mixture forms a ball.

Turn on floured board; knead until dough is smooth and elastic; cut into quarters.

Roll quartered dough, one part at a time, into a rectangular shape about ⅛ inch thick; cut first into pencil-thin strips, then into 1-inch pieces.

Drop into slightly salted boiling water; cook until dumplings rise to the surface. Simmer until tender, about 5 minutes; drain. Serve in a hot dish.

Grytstek ★

(Swedish Pot Roast)

Total Time: about 3 hours   Serves: 8 or more

- ¼ pound salt pork
- 3- to 4-pound boneless beef pot roast
- Salt and white pepper to taste
- 2 tablespoons butter or margarine
- ½ cup chopped onions
- 6 peppercorns
- 1 bay leaf, crushed
- 2 anchovy fillets, chopped fine
- ¼ cup chopped dill pickles
- ½ teaspoon sugar
- ½ to ¾ cup hot beef bouillon or consommé
- 3 to 4 yellow turnips, scraped and sliced
- 3 to 4 carrots, scraped and quartered
- 6 to 8 small potatoes of uniform size, peeled
- 1 cup (or more) light cream
- 1 teaspoon (or more) flour
- Nutmeg to taste
- Minced dill to taste

Cut salt pork into 2-inch slices; cut slices into ¼-inch strips; roll in very little salt and pepper. Cut about twelve incisions into meat; press one pork strip into each. Tie meat with string.

In Dutch oven or heavy skillet, melt butter; brown meat slowly on all sides, about 15 minutes; mix in onions. Stir the five seasonings into hot bouillon; pour over meat.

Cover tightly. Braise over low heat for 2 hours; turn and baste meat occasionally.

Add the three vegetables; cover and simmer until meat and vegetables are tender, about ½ hour. Remove meat and vegetables to hot platter; keep hot.

To make gravy: Strain meat juices if desired, and measure. For each 2 cups, add 1 cup cream and 1 teaspoon flour. Simmer gravy over low heat until slightly thickened and well blended; add salt and pepper to taste.

To serve: Slice meat; spoon part of gravy over meat; serve remaining gravy in separate dish. Sprinkle turnips lightly with nutmeg, toss carrots and potatoes in minced dill; serve vegetables in separate dishes.

Creole Pot Roast ★

Total Time:
bone-in meat,
about 2½–3½ hours;
boneless meat, 3–4 hours

Serves:
bone-in meat, 6 or more
boneless meat, 8 or more

    3 tablespoons meat fat, bacon drippings or shortening
    3- to 4-pound beef pot roast
    1 teaspoon salt
    ¼ teaspoon black pepper
    ½ cup chopped onions
    ½ cup sliced green olives
    2 chopped canned pimientos
    1 can (10½ ounces) condensed tomato soup,
        undiluted
    ½ cup sherry
    4 drops Tabasco

In Dutch oven, heavy skillet, or casserole, heat fat; brown meat slowly on all sides, about 15 minutes; pour off excess fat. Sprinkle with salt, pepper, onion, olives, and pimiento. Mix tomato soup with wine; pour over meat; blend well.

Cover tightly. Braise either on top of stove or in a moderate (350° F.) oven until meat is tender, about 2½ to 3 hours. Stir in Tabasco before serving.

Serve with fluffy rice and buttered carrots or green beans.

Boeuf Provençal ★

This traditional French pot roast may be served hot or cold. Glaze one day before serving cold.

Total Time: about 3 hours   Serves: 8 or more

    3- to 4-pound beef round or rolled boned (chuck)
    2 cut cloves garlic
Salt and black pepper to taste
    3 to 4 tablespoons bacon drippings
    2 cups chopped onions
    4 carrots, scraped and sliced
    1 celery stalk, chopped
    2 peppercorns
    2 whole cloves
    ½ teaspoon grated lemon or orange peel
    1 cup (or more) hot bouillon or consommé
    ½ cup (or more) red wine

Rub meat with garlic, salt and pepper.

In Dutch oven or heavy skillet, heat bacon drippings; brown meat slowly on all sides, about 15 minutes.

Cover with onions, carrots and celery. Stir peppercorns, cloves and grated peel into bouillon mixed with wine; pour over meat. Cover tightly. Braise over very low heat until meat is tender, about 2 to 3 hours.

Remove meat; if tied, take off string. Cool sauce to remove fat.

To serve hot: Place meat on hot platter; reheat sauce if necessary and serve in separate dish.

To serve cold: Place meat on cold platter; slowly spoon cold sauce over meat to cover. Let cool. The sauce will form a clear, soft jelly.

Serve with baked or scalloped potatoes and a plain salad. In France, no other vegetable is served.

Hungarian Gypsy Pot Roast ★

Total Time: Serves:
bone-in meat,   bone-in meat, 6 or more;
about 2½–3½ hours;   boneless meat, 8 or more
boneless meat, 3–4 hours

    3- to 4-pound beef pot roast
    2 tablespoons meat fat or bacon drippings
    ½ cup chopped onions
 1¼ cups stewed tomatoes
    2 teaspoons Hungarian paprika
    ½ teaspoon (or more) salt
    ¼ teaspoon white or black pepper
    ½ cup red wine or bouillon
    1 cup dried pitted prunes
    1 cup dried apricots
 1½ cups hot water

In Dutch oven or heavy skillet, heat meat until 2 table-spoons of melted fat have collected; if there is no excess fat on meat, add bacon drippings. Brown meat slowly on all sides about 15 minutes. Add onions, tomatoes, paprika, salt, pepper and wine; blend well. Cover tightly. Braise 1 hour.

At the same time, soak dried fruits in hot water for 1 hour; drain, and reserve liquid.

Place fruits on meat. Cover tightly. Braise until meat is tender, about 1 to 1½ hours for bone-in meat and 1½ to 2 hours for boneless meat. Baste after 1 hour. Add hot fruit liquid in small quantities if needed.

Remove meat; slice after 10 minutes; return to cooker and reheat if necessary.

To serve: Place in hot serving bowl with hot buttered egg noodles and a crusty bread.

Cranberry Pot Roast ★

Total Time: Serves:
bone-in meat,   bone-in meat, 6 or more;
about 2½–3 hours;   boneless meat, 8 or more
boneless meat, 3–4 hours

3 tablespoons butter or bacon drippings
3- to 4-pound beef pot roast
2 teaspoons salt
1 can (1 pound) whole or jellied cranberry sauce
½ cup hot beef bouillon or sherry
½ teaspoon cinnamon
¼ teaspoon cloves
⅛ teaspoon garlic powder, or 1 clove garlic, mashed or puréed

In Dutch oven or casserole, heat butter; brown meat slowly on all sides, about 15 minutes; pour off excess fat; sprinkle with salt.

Mix cranberry sauce with bouillon, cinnamon, cloves and garlic; pour over meat.

Cover tightly. Braise over very low heat on top of stove or in a slow (325° F.) oven until meat is tender: about 2 to 2½ hours for bone-in meat and 2½ to 3½ hours for boneless meat.

Serve with baked or jacket potatoes or steamed corn on cob; and a bowl of tossed green salad. *NOTE:* If desired, six to eight small peeled potatoes may be added 45 minutes before roast is tender. In such case, serve with tossed salad only.

Bavarian Beef Shanks with Horseradish Sauce ★

Total Time: about 2½ hours   Serves: 4 to 6

    2 pounds cross-cut beef shanks
    1 tablespoon salt
    2 bay leaves
    6 whole cloves
    1 large celery stalk, cut up
    1 to 1¼ cups beer or water
    6 medium-sized potatoes, peeled and halved
    4 medium-sized onions, peeled and halved
    3 large carrots, scraped and quartered
Quick Horseradish Sauce recipe

Place meat in Dutch oven or heavy skillet; add the three seasonings, celery and beer; blend and bring to quick boil.

Cover tightly. Braise over very low heat until meat is almost tender, about 2 hours.

Add the three vegetables. Cover and simmer until vegetables and meat are tender, about 25 minutes.

To serve: Drain meat and vegetables; place on hot platter. Serve with Quick Horseradish Sauce in separate dish.

NOTE: Use liquid as soup or in the preparation of other dishes.

Quick Horseradish Sauce

Total Time: about 30 minutes   Yield: about 1¼ cups
                                       sauce

Blend together ¼ cup bottled drained horseradish, 1 cup sour cream and ½ teaspoon dry mustard. Chill for at least 20 minutes before serving.

BEEF STEAKS

Thrift-cut steaks can be served like other steaks: broiled or grilled indoors and outdoors; pan-broiled and pan-fried. For broiling, many thrift cuts need tenderizing; see *Seven Ways to Make Meat Tender Before Cooking* on page 9. Thicker steaks are at their very best when braised.

How to Plan Beef Steak Servings

ONE AVERAGE SERVING	POUNDS PER SERVING
Bone-in meat	⅓–¾
Boneless meat	¼–½

For step-by-step directions to refrigerate and freeze fresh steaks, see *Meat Storage in Transit*. Cooked steaks should not be frozen; it is best to use leftovers soon. Braised steaks may be reheated. See also *Carving Made Easy*.

Cuts to Select for Beef Steaks

The lean should be red in color and firm in texture, with streaks of marbling; and the fat should be firm and creamy white.

Round steak: large, oval-shaped with small round bone; sometimes available in the three cuts shown below.

Round steak

Top round steak: the more tender boneless part, nearly all lean meat; usually cut ½ to 1½ inches thick.

Top round steak

Bottom round steak: the less tender boneless part; usually cut ½ inch thick; thicker for Swiss Steak.

Bottom round steak

Eye round steak: the smallest of the three cuts.

Eye of round

Rump steak: sometimes called "Swiss Steak"; a flavorful cut, usually boned.

Sirloin tip steak: lean and boneless.

Sirloin tip steak

Shoulder steak: cut from shoulder pot roast; with round bone in, or boneless.

Boneless shoulder steak

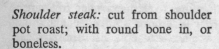

Chuck steak: with round or blade bone, or boneless; sometimes named Arm Steak, Blade Steak or Chicken Steak.

Chuck steak

Chicken steaks

Flank steak: the boneless, flat-muscle classic steak for London Broil.

Flank steak

Minute or cubed steak: small, thin, lean steak from round of chuck, ¼ to ½ inch thick; scored and cubed by machine.

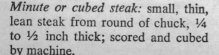

Minute or cube steak

Broiled Beef Steaks
(Basic Recipe)

For steaks 1-inch thick or more:

Keep at room temperature for 30 minutes before cooking, if possible.

1. Trim excess fat from steak; slash fat edge every 2 inches to prevent curling and "cupping." Brush very lean steaks with oil. Tenderize if necessary; no tenderizing for high-quality top round, flank (London Broil) and chicken steaks, and minute or cubed steaks.

2. Set oven regulator for broiling. Preheat broiler for 10 minutes.

3. Place steak on rack. Insert rack in broiler pan which has been lined with foil. The thickness of the steak and the desired degree of doneness determine its distance from the source of heat and length of broiling time.

THICKNESS OF STEAK	DISTANCE FROM HEAT
1 inch	about 3 inches
2 inches	about 4 to 6 inches

4. Broil one side for about one-half of total broiling time. Turn with tongs. Broil second side to desired doneness; see chart below.

To test doneness: With a sharp knife, cut a slit into meat near bone or in center of steak. Check color. A red color is for rare, pink for medium, and brown for well done.

5. Season to taste. Serve steak at once on hot platter.

Serve steaks with salt and freshly ground pepper; your favorite meat sauce, such as Worcestershire sauce, a bottled thick meat sauce, or Tabasco; butter or margarine, plain or mixed with prepared mustard, anchovy paste, Roquefort or blue cheese; broiled mushrooms or broiled tomato halves.

All broiled steaks may be cooked outdoors. Follow the cooker's directions.

Guide to
Broiling Time for Beef Steaks

THICKNESS OF STEAK	BROILING TIME IN MINUTES PER SIDE		
	rare	medium	well done
1 inch	5–6	6–7	7–8
up to 1½ inches	9	10	12–13

For thicker steaks, increase broiling time by 5 minutes on each side.

NOTE: If a commercial instant meat tenderizer is used, reduce broiling time by one-fourth. *Example:* The total broiling time of a 1-inch-thick steak, well done, is 16 minutes (= 8 minutes × 2). For a tenderized steak, deduct ¼th of 16 = 4 minutes. Total broiling time with tenderizer is 12 minutes (= 16 minus 4), or 6 minutes on each side.

Pan-Broiled Beef Steaks
(Basic Recipe)

For steaks up to ¾ inch thick:

1. Trim excess fat from steak; slash fat edge every 2 inches to prevent curling. Tenderize if necessary; see *Seven Ways to Make Meat Tender.* Do not tenderize minute or cubed steaks.

2. Heat heavy skillet or ridged griddle. Rub lightly with very little oil or trimmed-off fat. Brown steak slowly on both sides. Turn with tongs. Add no water. Do not cover.

3. Reduce heat. Broil steak to desired doneness. Pan-broiling requires about one-half the time of oven-broiling; see above. Pour off fat as it accumulates. Do not overcook. Serve at once on hot platter.

Pan-Fried (Sautéed) Beef Steaks
(Basic Recipe)

For very thin, lean steaks:

1. In heavy skillet, brown meat in small amount of fat on both sides. Season. Reduce heat.

2. Cook uncovered. Add no water. Turn occasionally with tongs. Remove from pan when done. Serve at once.

Braised Beef Steaks ★
(Basic Recipe)

Total Time: One Serving:
45 minutes–3 hours   bone-in meat, ⅓–¾ pound
                               boneless meat, ¼–½ pound

1. Trim excess fat from steak; slash fat edge every 2 inches to prevent curling. Season to taste with plain celery, garlic or onion salt; and with black or white pepper. Sprinkle meat with flour and coat lightly; shake off excess flour. If steak is not coated with flour, season after browning.

2. In heavy skillet, casserole, or electric table cooker with tight-fitting cover, heat 1 or 2 tablespoons meat fat, bacon drippings, oil, butter, or margarine. Brown meat slowly on both sides, turning with tongs or pancake turner, about 15 to 20 minutes. Season uncoated meat.

3. Add ½ to 1 cup liquid (water, beef bouillon, wine, beer, tomato juice, or ginger ale). The exact quantity will depend on size of steak and pan.

4. Cover tightly. Braise slowly until steak is fork-tender, from 45 minutes to 2 or 3 hours depending on quality and thickness of meat; see chart below. Turn occasionally. Add more liquid as needed, a little at a time.

IMPORTANT: Larger steaks may be cooked ahead; follow step-by-step directions for the Basic Beef Pot Roast; and don't forget to set the timer to turn the steak.

5. If desired, add vegetables during the last 45 minutes of braising.

6. Serve steak on hot platter with meat juices in separate dish or make a thick gravy; see the Basic Beef Pot Roast, step 7. Serve soon. Slice steak at the table.

NOTE: Leftover steak may be reheated.

Guide to
Braising Time for Beef Steaks

THICKNESS OF STEAK	MINUTES
½-inch-thick steaks	40–45
¾-inch-thick round steaks	60–90
½- to ¾-inch-thick stuffed steaks	90
Swiss steaks, 1½- to 2½-inches thick	120–180

Broiled Beef Steak Béarnaise

Total Time: about 30 minutes   Serves: 6 or more
after tenderizing

2½-pound top round (chuck) steak, 1 inch thick
Seasoned meat tenderizer
2 tablespoons flour
Melted butter or margarine
Salt and black pepper to taste
Garlic powder, if desired
Béarnaise Sauce recipe

Set oven regulator for broiling; preheat broiler for 10 minutes. Trim excess fat from steak; slash fat edge at 1-inch intervals; tenderize as label directs.

Rub broiler rack with fat trimmed from steak or brush with oil.

Place steak on rack; sprinkle top with 1 tablespoon flour; brush lightly with butter. Insert rack in broiler pan lined with foil.

Broil steak, 3 to 4 inches below source of heat, for 3 to 4 minutes for rare, and 5 to 6 minutes for medium, doneness. Turn steak with tongs.

Sprinkle remaining flour over top of steak; brush lightly with butter. Broil second side 2 to 3 minutes for rare, and 3 to 4 minutes for medium, doneness.

Season to taste with salt, pepper and garlic powder. Spoon Béarnaise sauce over steak. Garnish with watercress, pickle fans, or radish roses. Serve at once with French fried or boiled potatoes and a mixed salad. *NOTE:* For outdoor cooking, baste with Spicy Barbecue sauce; see *Index* for recipe.

Bearnaise Sauce

Total Time: about 25 minutes   Yield: about 1 cup sauce

    3 tablespoons tarragon vinegar
    3 tablespoons water or bouillon
    3 onion slices
    2 egg yolks, slightly beaten
    ½ teaspoon salt
    ¼ teaspoon paprika
    4 tablespoons butter or margarine

In small saucepan, bring vinegar, water, and onion slices to a rolling boil; discard onion.

Place egg yolks in top of double boiler; gradually stir in slightly cooled vinegar mixture; add salt and paprika. Cook over hot water until mixture thickens; stir constantly.

Add butter, 1 tablespoon at a time, beating constantly until sauce is quite thick and creamy. Cover, and remove from heat.

Oven-Broiled Barbecue Steak

Total Time: Serves: about 6
to marinate: 2–3 hours or overnight;
to broil: about 30 minutes

Barbecue Sauce recipe
2-pound round steak, about 1½ inches thick

To marinate: Trim excess fat from steak; slash fat edge at 2-inch intervals, if necessary. Brush with Barbecue sauce and marinate for 2 to 3 hours or overnight. Remove sauce with spatula or the back of a knife before broiling; reserve sauce.

To broil: Set oven regulator for broiling. Preheat broiler for 10 minutes. Rub broiler rack with a little oil or bacon drippings. Place steak on rack. Insert rack in broiler pan lined with foil.

Broil steak 4 inches below source of heat for 5 minutes; spread with half the sauce and broil 10 minutes longer. Turn steak with tongs.

Broil other side for 5 minutes. Spread with sauce and broil to desired doneness. See page 36 for approximate broiling time.

Dot with remaining sauce. Serve at once with broiled tomato halves or buttered corn on the cob.

Barbecue Sauce ★
(uncooked)

Total Time: about   Yield: about 1½ cups sauce
30 minutes

   1 cup chili sauce
   ½ cup cider or wine vinegar
   2 tablespoons sugar
   2 tablespoons prepared mustard
   1 clove garlic, mashed or puréed, or ⅛ teaspoon
       garlic powder
   ½ teaspoon onion powder
   Salt and black pepper to taste

Blend ingredients in a bowl or jar. Let mixture rest for
about 25 minutes. Blend or shake first before use.

Outdoor-Grilled Barbecue Steak

Total Time: about 30 minutes   Serves: about 6

Use ingredients of Oven-Broiled Barbecue Steak. Double
quantity of barbecue sauce recipe.

Prepare grill as manufacturer directs. Place steak on
grill 6 to 8 inches above coals. Grill for 5 minutes. Turn
steak; spread thinly with sauce and grill for 10 more
minutes. Turn steak again; spread with sauce and grill
for 10 minutes or to desired doneness.
To serve: Spread with remaining sauce. Serve with
French fried potatoes and sliced tomatoes.

"True Blue" London Broil

Total Time: about 30 minutes   Serves: about 6

    2 to 2½ pounds top-quality flank steak
    1 teaspoon (or more) olive oil
    Salt and black pepper to taste
    Garlic powder, if desired

About 15 minutes before broiling, rub meat lightly on both sides with oil. Trim excess fat if needed. Using a sharp knife, lightly score the steak crosswise on both sides.

Set oven regulator for broiling. Preheat broiler for 10 minutes. Rub broiler rack with oil. Place steak on rack. Insert rack in broiler pan lined with foil.

Broil steak 4 inches below source of heat for 7 minutes. Turn with tongs. Broil other side for 5 minutes. Remove steak from oven. Season to taste with salt and pepper. Sprinkle with garlic, if desired.

Place steak on cutting board and let rest for 5 minutes. With a sharp knife slice across the grain of meat, cutting *very thin* slices almost parallel to the board.

Serve at once with French fried potatoes; steamed broccoli spears or green beans; and tomato slices in French dressing.

Cubed Steaks with Western Sauce

Total Time: about 15 minutes   Serves: 4

    4 cubed steaks
    3 tablespoons flour
    1 teaspoon salt (or less)
    ⅛ teaspoon black pepper
    Butter, margarine, or oil

Western Sauce:
- ½ cup catsup
- 2 tablespoons Worcestershire sauce
- 2 tablespoons lemon juice
- ½ teaspoon onion powder
- ½ teaspoon garlic powder or 1 clove garlic, mashed or puréed

Rub steaks with a mixture of flour, salt, and pepper; shake off excess.

Heat heavy skillet; coat lightly with butter. Brown steaks slowly on one side, about 2 to 3 minutes, until a light crust forms. Turn with tongs and brown other side. Remove immediately to hot platter.

Add sauce ingredients to fat left in skillet. Bring mixture to boil, stirring constantly; spoon over steaks.

Serve at once with scalloped potatoes or succotash.

French-Dressed Cubed Steaks

Total Time: Serves: 4
before cooking, 1 hour;
for cooking, about 15 minutes

- 4 cubed steaks
- 1 teaspoon salt
- ⅛ teaspoon black pepper
- ⅛ teaspoon garlic powder
- ½ cup French dressing
- Butter or margarine

To marinate: One hour before serving, sprinkle steaks on both sides with a mixture of salt, pepper, and garlic. Place steaks on a platter; cover with dressing. Cover with waxed paper; place a weight, such as a heavy platter, on top. Marinate 30 minutes. Turn steaks; cover again and marinate for another 30 minutes.

To cook: Heat heavy skillet. Rub lightly with butter.

Brown steaks slowly, about 2 to 3 minutes on each side.
Turn with tongs.

Spoon remaining dressing over steaks. Serve at once
with baked potatoes and buttered wax beans or asparagus.

Minute Steak au Poivre
(A French Classic)

A very strong, peppery steak.   Serves: 4
Total Time: about 20 minutes

    4 cubed steaks
    Freshly ground coarse black pepper
    4 tablespoons butter or margarine
    1 tablespoon olive oil
    3 tablespoons brandy
    ¼ cup white wine
    Salt to taste, at the table

Ten minutes before broiling, press pepper firmly into
steaks with hands or rolling pin, in quantity to taste.

In heavy skillet, heat 3 tablespoons butter and olive
oil; brown steaks quickly, about 2 minutes on each side.
Steaks must be rare.

Add brandy; light with match. When the flames die
out, remove steaks at once to hot platter.

Add remaining 1 tablespoon butter and wine to butter
in skillet. Let come to quick boil. Pour sauce over steaks.

Serve at once with French bread and Caesar salad.
Steaks are salted at the table.

Swiss Steak ★

Total Time: about 3 hours   Serves: 4 or more

1½ pounds (bottom round or rump) beef steak, 1½ inches thick
½ cup flour
1 teaspoon salt
¼ teaspoon black pepper
⅛ teaspoon dried thyme
2 tablespoons oil, butter, or margarine
1 cup chopped onions
½ cup chopped green peppers
½ cup sherry or wine
½ cup water

Trim excess fat from steak; slash fat edge at 2-inch intervals, if needed.

Blend flour with salt, pepper, and thyme; pound into steak on both sides until all flour is used.

In heavy skillet, heat oil. Brown meat slowly on both sides, about 15 to 20 minutes; turn with tongs. Add remaining ingredients and blend well.

Cover tightly. Braise over low heat or bake, uncovered, in a moderate (350° F) oven, until meat is tender, about 2 to 2½ hours. Do not baste. *NOTE:* If desired, add canned kernel corn or peas during the last 30 minutes of braising.

Remove steak to hot platter. Skim fat off meat juices if necessary and simmer 5 minutes. Pour juices over meat.

Serve at once with mashed or baked potatoes and a tossed green salad.

Spanish Beef Steak ★

For sherry and water in Swiss Steak recipe, substitute 2 cups stewed tomatoes and ⅛ teaspoon dried oregano.

Barbecued Flank Steak ★
(A Braised Steak)

Total Time: about 3 hours   Serves: 6 or more

    1 2½-pound flank steak, scored into diamond shapes
    2 teaspoons salt
    ½ teaspoon black pepper

Barbecue Sauce (uncooked):
    ¼ cup catsup
    ¼ cup lemon juice or cider vinegar
    2 tablespoons brown sugar
    ¼ teaspoon garlic powder or juice
    ¼ teaspoon dry mustard
    1 can (8 ounces) tomato sauce
    ½ cup beef bouillon or red wine

    2 tablespoons (or more) flour
    Worcestershire sauce to taste

Trim excess fat from meat.

In Dutch oven or heavy skillet, brown meat on both sides in its own fat for about 10 minutes; sprinkle with salt and pepper. Mix ingredients of barbecue sauce; pour over meat.

Cover tightly. Braise over low heat until almost tender, about 2 hours; turn meat once or twice with tongs during braising. Remove meat to hot platter; keep hot.

To make gravy: Skim most fat off meat juices; add enough water to make 2 cups. Blend flour with 3 tablespoons meat juices to a smooth paste. Stir into liquid in cooker. Simmer until slightly thickened, stirring frequently.

Add meat; cover and simmer until tender, about 15 to 30 minutes. Season with Worcestershire sauce.

To serve: Slice meat on the diagonal and cover with sauce. Serve at once with a yellow or green vegetable and crusty bread or jacket potatoes.

Creamed Mushroom Steak

Total Time: about 1¾ hours   Serves: 4 or more

- 1 shoulder beef steak, about 1½ pounds
- ¼ cup flour
- ½ teaspoon salt
- ¼ teaspoon white or black pepper
- 1 tablespoon olive oil, butter, or margarine
- 1 can (10½ ounces) condensed cream of mushroom soup, undiluted
- 1 can (8 ounces) mushroom stems and pieces, undrained
- ¼ cup sherry
- 1 cup chopped celery stalks and leaves
- 1 tablespoon minced parsley or chives

If necessary, slash edges of steak at 2-inch intervals. Mix flour with salt and pepper; rub thoroughly into meat.

In heavy skillet or casserole, heat oil. Brown steak slowly on both sides about 15 minutes.

In small bowl, mix mushroom soup, mushrooms, sherry, and celery; blend well. Pour over steak; bring to quick boil.

Cover tightly; reduce heat. Braise 45 minutes. Turn steak with tongs and braise until meat is tender, about 30 to 40 minutes.

Sprinkle with parsley. Serve piping hot with steamed carrots and a mixed green salad.

Flank Steak Roulades
(Stuffed Flank Steak)

Total Time: about 2½ hours   Serves: 4 or more

- 1 2-pound flank steak, scored in diamond shapes and cut in 4-inch squares
- 1 cup chopped onions
- 2 canned pimientos, chopped
- 1 teaspoon prepared (yellow) mustard
- ½ teaspoon salt
- ¼ teaspoon dried oregano
- 2 tablespoons bacon drippings or oil
- 2 cups stewed tomatoes
- ½ cup sherry or water
- 3 to 4 cups hot buttered spaghetti

Place steak squares on board. In small bowl, blend onions with pimiento, mustard, salt, and oregano; spoon evenly on steak squares. Roll up in jelly roll fashion; secure with skewers or strings.

In heavy skillet or casserole, heat bacon drippings. Brown meat slowly and evenly on all sides, about 15 minutes.

Add tomatoes blended with sherry. Cover tightly. Braise over low heat on top of stove or in a moderate (350° F.) oven until meat is tender, about 2 hours.

Remove skewers or strings. Season meat juices if needed.

Serve on bed of buttered spaghetti and with a tossed green salad.

Stuffed Cubed Beef Steaks

Total Time: about 1½ hours   Serves: 6

    6 thin cubed beef steaks
    ½ cup chopped onions
    ¼ teaspoon (or more) garlic powder
    2 teaspoons prepared mustard
    6 tablespoons butter or margarine
    1 can (10½ ounces) consommé
    ½ cup white wine
    Minced chives or dill

Place steaks on board. In small bowl, mix onions with garlic and mustard; spread on steaks. Roll up tightly in jelly roll fashion; secure with skewers or strings.

In heavy skillet, heat butter. Brown steaks slowly on all sides, about 10 minutes. Add consommé blended with wine. Cover tightly.

Braise slowly over low heat until tender, about 60 minutes. Do not baste.

To serve: Remove skewers or strings; sprinkle with chives. Serve with buttered wax beans or mixed vegetables; and a creamy cole slaw.

Beef Sukiyaki

In the Orient, this dish is usually prepared at the table. It can be cooked at the table or in the back yard, either in a heat-controlled electric skillet or in a skillet set over a hibachi.

Total Time: about 1 hour   Serves: 6 or more
Actual cooking: about 10 minutes

Sukiyaki Sauce:
    ¾ cup soy sauce
    1 to 1½ cups chicken broth
    ¼ cup sake or white wine
    3 tablespoons sugar

Sukiyaki:
    1 pound thin beef steak, top round or prime-quality
        chuck, very thinly sliced into 2 × ¼-inch strips
    3 celery stalks, cut diagonally into ½-inch pieces
    1 large white onion, thinly sliced
    1 bunch green onions, cut in 2-inch pieces lengthwise
    1 cup sliced fresh mushrooms
    1 can (8½ ounces) bamboo shoots, drained and sliced
    1 can (1 pound) soybean sprouts, rinsed and drained

About 1 hour before cooking, blend sauce ingredients in a pitcher; cover and set aside.

Shortly before cooking, arrange meat and all vegetables on a platter or tray; set aside.

If an electric skillet is used, set temperature control at high or as manufacturer directs. Otherwise, heat heavy skillet; set on hibachi, if desired.

Rub heated skillet with 2 tablespoons sauce. With a long fork, place about one-half the meat in the center of the skillet and about one-half of the vegetables in a circle around it. Pour one-fourth of the sauce over it.

Cook quickly for 2 minutes, turning meat pieces once. Reduce heat to medium and panbroil for 5 to 8 minutes. Add a few tablespoons sauce if needed. Press foods gently into sauce from time to time. Do not overcook.

Remove finished food to plates. Cook remaining food as above and serve as the meal proceeds.

Serve with hot steamed rice and green tea, if desired.

Beef Chow Mein

Total Time: about 1 hour   Serves: 6 to 8

1½-pound round beef steak, cut into 1-inch strips
2 tablespoons butter or oil
1½ cups beef bouillon or
¾ cup each of white wine and water
1 teaspoon ginger
¼ teaspoon garlic powder
¼ cup soy sauce
2 tablespoons cornstarch
¼ cup cold water
1 can (1 pound) soybean sprouts, rinsed and drained
1 can (1 pound) Chinese vegetables, undrained
3 to 4 cups hot fluffy rice
1 can (3 ounces) chow mein noodles

Trim fat from meat, if necessary. In heavy skillet, heat butter. Brown meat on all sides, about 10 minutes. Add bouillon, ginger, garlic and soy sauce; blend well.

Cover tightly. Braise over low heat until meat is tender, about 30 minutes.

Blend cornstarch with water until smooth; stir into chow mein until thickened and clear.

Add sprouts and vegetables. Cover and simmer until vegetables are heated and meat is tender, about 15 minutes.

Serve at once on bed of hot rice, with chow mein noodles in separate dish.

Beef Stroganoff—Russian Style

Total Time: about 45 minutes   Serves: 4 to 6

1½-pound top round or sirloin tip beef steak
¼ cup flour
1 teaspoon salt
4 tablespoons butter or margarine
½ cup chopped onions
1 clove garlic, mashed or puréed
½ teaspoon black pepper
1 can (10½ ounces) bouillon or consommé
¼ cup sherry or water, if needed
1 can (4 ounces) mushroom pieces and stems, undrained
1 cup sour cream (at room temperature)
3 cups shoestring potatoes, cooked or canned
1 tablespoon minced fresh dill or
½ teaspoon dried dill weeds

Trim excess fat from meat; cut diagonally into thin strips, about 2 inches long; roll strips in flour blended with salt.

In heavy skillet, melt butter; add meat and brown on all sides, about 10 minutes. Turn often.

Add onions, garlic, pepper and bouillon; blend well.

Cover tightly. Braise over low heat until meat is tender, about 20 minutes. Add up to ¼ cup wine if necessary.

Blend mushrooms with sour cream; stir into meat mixture; heat through gently, but do not boil. Sprinkle with dill.

Serve immediately with shoestring potatoes and sliced dill pickles in separate dishes.

Beef Stroganoff—Hungarian Style

Total Time: about 45 minutes   Serves: about 4

- 1-pound top round beef steak
- 4 tablespoons butter or margarine
- ½ cup chopped onions
- 1 can (10½ ounces) condensed tomato soup
- ½ cup sherry or red wine
- ½ pound sliced mushrooms
- 1 tablespoon flour
- 1 tablespoon Hungarian paprika
- 1 teaspoon salt
- 1 teaspoon sugar
- 1 teaspoon dry mustard
- 1 teaspoon lemon juice
- 1 teaspoon cider or wine vinegar
- ¼ teaspoon black pepper
- 1 cup sour cream, if desired
- 3 cups hot buttered egg noodles

Trim excess fat from meat; cut diagonally into thin, narrow strips, about 2 inches long.

In heavy skillet, heat butter; add meat and brown on all sides, turning often, about 10 minutes; add onions and sauté until golden, about 5 minutes; stir often.

Add soup, wine and mushrooms; blend well. Cover tightly. Braise over low heat for 15 minutes.

Blend flour into ⅓ cup meat juices; add the seven seasonings in the order given; mix well and stir into meat mixture. Simmer, uncovered, for about 5 minutes or until sauce thickens lightly; stir occasionally.

If desired, blend ½ cup gravy with sour cream (at room temperature); stir into meat mixture; heat gently, but do not boil.

Serve at once on bed of noodles, with spiced fruit or a tossed green salad.

BEEF STEWS

Men like stews for their tender morsels of meat and flavorful gravy. Thrifty gourmet cooks know six more good reasons.

1. The least expensive meat cuts oftentimes make the tastiest stews;

2. Stews are table-ready in about 1½ hours (depending on the cut used, its quality, and the size of the meat cubes), with no pot-watching;

3. Most leftovers "hanging around" in the refrigerator may be added to good advantage: fresh or canned vegetables, strained baby foods (carrots, beans, spinach, liver, etc.), tomato juice and soup stock—even a few tablespoons of mashed potatoes, can be used instead of flour to thicken a stew's gravy;

4. Imaginative seasoning comes easy with stews, as many cooks can tell;

5. Even the best stews improve by reheating. As said before, stews can and should be cooked at least one day before serving;

6. Without potatoes, stews freeze very well. When frozen in freezer-to-oven-to-table cookware, they reheat in a slow (325° F.) oven and can be served in the same dish.

For step-by-step directions to refrigerate or freeze fresh stew meat and cooked stews, see *Meat Storage in Transit*.

How to Plan Beef Stew Servings

Count about 6 servings in 2 pounds boneless beef. It is advisable, however, to make stews with no less than 2 to 3 pounds of meat; and allow for extra helpings or the most desirable leftovers.

Cuts to Select for Beef Stew

Packaged "stewing beef," usually boneless meat in 1- or 2-inch pieces cut from less-tender meat. Good quality meat is bright red with almost white fat. Avoid stewing beef with too much fat in proportion to its lean. Excess fat would have to be skimmed off after braising, and you would end up with less meat on the platter. "Stewing beef" with some small bones, though excellent in flavor, is usually less economical in terms of actual servings.

Any piece of boneless or boned beef, cut into cubes of fairly uniform size by the meatman or yourself. Meat cubes should be 1½ inches or 2 inches in size so that they become tender at the same time. However, do not waste meat trying to cut cubes of perfect identical size.

Other flavorful cuts for beef stew are the lean pieces of shoulder (chuck), bottom round, flank, shin, shank and neck; also fresh brisket, plate and heel of round. Shank and neck meat will need slightly longer braising.

The Basic Beef Stew ★

Total Time: about 2 hours   Serves: 6 or more

    2 to 3 pounds boneless stewing beef, cut in 1½- or
        2-inch cubes
    2 tablespoons fat or oil
    1 to 1½ cups liquid (bouillon, wine, soup stock, left-
        over meat juices, or water)
    Vegetables (optional)
    Thickened gravy (optional)
    For brown stews only:
    ½ cup flour
     2 teaspoons salt
    ¼ teaspoon black pepper
    ⅛ teaspoon paprika (optional)
    ½ teaspoon sugar

1. Select a Dutch oven, heavy skillet, or casserole with
tight-fitting cover; or an electric table cooker or pressure
cooker.

2. Trim excess fat from meat. Brown or do not brown
meat, as desired.

For a brown stew: Blend flour and seasonings (except
sugar) in paper or plastic bag. Add a few pieces of meat
at a time; shake to coat evenly. To brown: Heat fat in
cooker; add meat; sprinkle with sugar to enhance browning. Turn cubes with tongs and sauté slowly on all sides,
about 15 minutes. It may be necessary to brown one-half
of the meat at a time and remove it to a hot platter. After
all meat is browned, pour off excess fat before returning
the meat cubes to cooker.

For a white stew: Sauté meat cubes in hot fat until they
lose their bright red color. Turn with tongs; pour off excess
fat. Add 2 teaspoons salt, ¼ teaspoon black pepper and
¼ teaspoon paprika.

3. Start braising. Add enough liquid to keep meat moist.
Cover cooker tightly. Braise over very low heat on top

of stove or in a slow (350° F.) oven, an electric table cooker or a pressure saucepan. Note the time. Set your portable timer and take it with you when you leave the kitchen.

If stew is to be served immediately after cooking: Braise meat until "fork-tender," that is, well done when pierced with a fork. Braising time will be about 1½ hours. If desired, add fresh vegetables after 1 hour of cooking and canned vegetables about 15 minutes before serving. Set your timer accordingly.

4. *To serve:* Spoon piping hot stew into a deep preheated serving dish; surround with vegetables; sprinkle with minced parsley or chives, and dust lightly with paprika.

5. *If stew is cooked ahead:* Braise only until "firm–tender," that is, some 15 minutes less than total cooking time. Do not add vegetables. Cool and refrigerate stew immediately; follow step-by-step directions on page 11.

To serve: About 45 minutes before serving, remove stew from refrigerator. Lift fat from top. Reheat only the quantity needed; refrigerate remaining stew immediately, as before.

One-half hour before serving, spoon stew into a heavy skillet. Cover and simmer over very low heat on top of stove until thoroughly heated. If desired, add canned vegetables after 15 minutes. Check seasoning.

6. *To make a thick gravy,* if desired: Drain meat and vegetables (if any) and remove to hot platter; keep hot. Blend 1 tablespoon flour with 3 to 4 tablespoons water; stir into meat juices and simmer for 5 minutes. Season to taste; return meat and any vegetables to reheat.

Vegetables for stews to serve separately or braise with the meat: scraped or peeled potatoes, quartered carrots, kernel corn, onions, peas, yellow or white (quartered) turnips, fresh or canned tomatoes.

Seasonings for stews: Good flavor combinations are:
—½ bay leaf and ¼ teaspoon of either dried marjoram,

oregano, thyme, basil, curry powder, or dill weeds;
—2 (or more) whole cloves or peppercorns;
—⅛ teaspoon garlic powder or 1 mashed clove garlic;
—a dash of pickling spices;
—1 teaspoon tarragon vinegar or 1 to 2 tablespoons red
wine.

Hungarian Beef Gulyas ★

Total Time: about 2 hours   Serves: 8 or more

    3 pounds boneless beef chuck, cut in 2-inch cubes
    ½ cup lard or bacon drippings
    4 cups chopped onions, about 1½ pounds
    1 tablespoon Hungarian paprika
    1 tablespoon salt (or less to taste)
    ½ teaspoon dried marjoram
    ½ teaspoon caraway seeds
    1 crumbled bay leaf
    3 large tomatoes, quartered
    1 green pepper, cut up (including core, seeds and
       stem)
    1 large square piece cheesecloth
    1 cup beef bouillon or water
    ½ cup red wine
    4 large potatoes, peeled and diced
    1 tablespoon lard or bacon drippings

Trim excess fat from meat. In Dutch oven or heavy skillet, heat lard. Add onions; sauté over low heat to a golden
brown, stirring frequently, about 10 minutes. Add paprika
and cook for 2 minutes, stirring constantly.

Add meat, salt, marjoram, caraway seeds, and bay leaf;
sauté until meat loses its red color, about 10 minutes. Turn
meat and onions frequently.

Meanwhile, put tomatoes and pepper on cheesecloth;
tie into a bag with a long string. Add to meat mixture

with string end outside of pot. Add bouillon and wine; bring to boil. Cover tightly. Reduce heat immediately.

Braise over low heat for 1 hour and 10 minutes. Add potatoes and continue braising until meat and potatoes are tender, about 20 minutes. Remove cheesecloth bag. Blend 1 tablespoon heated lard with 1 tablespoon paprika and ¼ cup meat juices. Stir into gulyas.

Serve with hot buttered noodles.

NOTE: If more gravy is desired, add ½ cup red wine or bouillon together with the potatoes.

Budapest Beef Gulyas with Teaspoon Dumplings ★

Total Time: about 2¼ hours   Serves: 6 to 8

  3 pounds boneless shin (beef), cut in 1½-inch cubes
 ¼ cup lard or bacon drippings
  4 cups chopped onions, about 1½ pounds
  2 tablespoons Hungarian paprika
  1 tablespoon salt
 ½ teaspoon black pepper
 ½ teaspoon caraway or celery seeds
  1 green pepper, chopped
  1 carrot, scraped and sliced
  1 celery stalk, diced
  1 cup red wine

Teaspoon Dumplings:
½ cup flour
 1 egg, beaten
 3 parsley sprigs, tied

Trim excess fat from meat. In heavy skillet or Dutch oven, heat lard; add onions and sauté until golden, about 10 minutes. Add paprika and meat; sauté about 15 minutes, turning frequently. Add remaining ingredients in order given, blending after each addition.

Cover tightly. Braise over low heat until meat is tender, about 1¾ hours.

Meanwhile, prepare dumplings: mix flour and egg to a stiff dough; drop by teaspoons into a pot of boiling water; add parsley. Cover and simmer until dumplings rise to the surface, about 10 minutes. Turn off heat; keep dumplings in cooking water until ready to serve; discard parsley. *NOTE:* If gulyas is cooked ahead, cook dumplings shortly before serving.

Serve gulyas with dumplings and a tossed green salad or creamy cole slaw.

Boeuf en Daube ★
(French Beef Stew)

Total Time: about 1¾ hours   Serves: about 6

- 4 bacon slices
- 2 pounds boneless lean stewing beef, cut in 1½-inch cubes
- Flour
- 1 clove garlic, put on toothpick or string
- ½ cup hot soup stock or water
- ½ cup red wine
- ½ teaspoon salt
- 18 (or more) small onions, peeled
- 1 cup diced green pepper
- 1 cup diced carrots
- 4 peppercorns
- 2 whole cloves
- 1 bay leaf

This is a famous dish in northern France. *En daube* means that vegetables are braised with the meat.

In large heavy skillet, sauté bacon until soft and light brown; drain on paper and cut into bite-size pieces.

Dredge meat with flour; sauté in bacon fat to brown evenly, about 10 minutes. Add garlic; sauté 5 minutes and remove.

Add soup stock and wine; bring to quick boil. Reduce heat. Add remaining ingredients and bacon pieces.

Cover tightly. Braise until meat is tender, about 1½ hours. Serve with crusty French bread and a Chef's salad.

Boeuf Bourguignon ★
(Beef Stew in Burgundy Wine)

Total Time: about 1¾ hours   Serves: 6 to 8

¼ pound diced salt pork or bacon
¼ cup flour (about)
½ tablespoon (or less) salt
Dash of black pepper
3 pounds lean beef chuck, cut in 1½-inch cubes
1 cup chopped onions
1½ cups sliced carrots
1 cup Burgundy or dry red wine
1 cup bouillon or consommé
1 can (8 ounces) mushroom stems and pieces, undrained
3 to 4 cups hot buttered noodles

Bouquet Garni:
3 sprigs parsley
1 small celery stalk, cut up
1 bay leaf
⅛ teaspoon dried marjoram or thyme

In heavy skillet, sauté salt pork for 5 minutes; remove and reserve. Mix flour with salt and pepper. Dredge meat with flour.

Sauté meat, onions, and carrots in fat, turning frequently, about 10 minutes. Add wine, bouillon, and the bouquet garni (tied in cheesecloth with long string end tied to handle of skillet). Bring to quick boil; reduce heat.

Cover tightly. Braise over low heat until meat is tender, about 1½ hours. Remove bouquet garni. Add mushrooms and reheat.

To serve: Place stew on bed of hot noodles in deep

serving dish. Serve with steamed squash or corn; and a tossed green salad with French dressing.

Carbonnade de Boeuf Flammande ★
(Sliced Beef and Beer Stew)

Total Time: about 2 hours   Serves: 6 or more

  3 pounds lean beef, boned neck or thin flank
  ¼ cup lard or fat
  2 teaspoons salt
  2 cups chopped onions
  2 tablespoons flour
  1 bottle or can (12 ounces) beer or ale (more if needed)
  ⅛ teaspoon black pepper
  1 teaspoon sugar
  ⅛ teaspoon garlic powder
  1 tablespoon wine or cider vinegar

Bouquet Garni:
  ⅓ teaspoon each of marjoram, rosemary, and thyme (dried or fresh, chopped)

Cut beef into strips about 1 inch thick and 2 inches long. In heavy (2-quart) casserole, heat fat. Sauté meat for 10 minutes, turning frequently. Sprinkle meat with 1 teaspoon salt; remove and reserve.

Sauté onions in same fat, about 5 minutes; turn frequently. Sprinkle with 1 teaspoon salt; remove and reserve. Drain off all but 2 tablespoons fat from cooker. Stir in flour until light brown. Gradually add beer; keep stirring until mixture comes to boil. Blend in pepper, sugar, garlic, and bouquet garni. Remove sauce and reserve.

In same casserole, arrange alternate layers of meat and onions. Cover with sauce. Cover casserole; bake in moderate (350° F.) oven for 1 hour.

Add ½ cup beer if necessary to keep meat mixture moist; continue baking for another 30 minutes.

Before serving, skim off fat and add vinegar. Serve in casserole with parslied new potatoes or rice in separate dish.

NOTE: Departing from the traditional layered stew, you may cook this stew on top of stove, blending the meat, onions, and sauce before braising.

Stifado ★
(Greek Beef Stew)

Total Time: about 2 hours   Serves: about 6

    2½ pounds stewing beef, cut in 1½-inch cubes
     4 tablespoons olive or salad oil
     1 can (8 ounces) tomato sauce
     1 cup red wine or beef bouillon
     3 tablespoons cider or tarragon vinegar
     2 teaspoons salt
    ½ teaspoon black pepper
     1 small stick cinnamon
     6 whole cloves
     2 cups chopped onions
    ½ cup chopped ripe olives
     3 to 4 cups hot steamed rice
        Minced parsley or chopped chives

Trim excess fat from meat. In Dutch oven or large heavy skillet, heat oil. Brown meat on all sides, about 15 minutes. Add tomato sauce mixed with wine, vinegar, salt, and pepper. Wrap cinnamon and cloves in cheesecloth; tie with long string and add to meat mixture with string end outside of cooker.

Add onions and olives; blend well. Cover tightly. Braise over low heat until meat is tender, about 1½ hours. Remove spice bag.

Serve the stew piping hot, with steamed rice in separate dish. Sprinkle meat and rice with parsley.

English Beef Stew with Fluffy Dumplings ★

Total Time: about 2 hours   Serves: 6 or more

- 2½ to 3 pounds stewing beef, cut in 1½-inch cubes
- 3 tablespoons butter or margarine
- 1 teaspoon sugar
- ¼ cup flour
- 3 cups beef bouillon or 1½ cups each white wine and water
- ¼ teaspoon white pepper
- ½ cup chopped onions
- 6 medium carrots, scraped and quartered
- 6 medium-sized potatoes, peeled and quartered

Seasoning Bouquet:
- 3 parsley sprigs
- 2 celery stalks, cut up
- 1 large slice onion
- 1 bay leaf
- 2 whole cloves

Dumplings:
- 1 egg
- 1 cup milk
- 2 cups biscuit mix

Trim excess fat from meat. In Dutch oven or (2½-quart) casserole, heat butter. Brown meat on all sides about 10 minutes. Sprinkle sugar on meat and continue to cook until meat is dark brown; stir constantly. Should the meat stick, shake the cooker.

Dust meat with flour; shake the cooker again until the flour is lightly browned. Add bouillon, salt, and pepper. Place seasoning bouquet in cheesecloth; tie with a long string; add to meat mixture with string end tied to handle of cooker. Bring mixture to quick boil. Reduce heat immediately. Cover tightly; braise for 1 hour.

Add vegetables; cover and braise for 15 minutes. Meanwhile, prepare dumplings: beat egg and milk together; stir quickly into biscuit mix. Drop dough by spoonfuls on top of stew. Cover tightly and simmer for 20 minutes without lifting the cover. Remove seasoning bag.

Serve immediately in casserole or transfer to hot serving dish. Serve with cucumber or a tossed green salad.

Canadian Beef-and-Onion Pie ★

Total Time: about 1¾ hours   Serves: about 6

      2 tablespoons bacon drippings or oil
      2 pounds stewing beef, cut in 1½-inch cubes
    ½ teaspoon salt
    ½ teaspoon Worcestershire sauce
    ¼ teaspoon black pepper
    ⅛ teaspoon dried thyme
      1 can (8 ounces) mushroom stems and pieces, undrained
      1 cup beef bouillon
      1 can or jar (16 ounces) boiled onions, drained
      4 cooked or canned potatoes, sliced or diced
    Pastry for Pie Crust recipe

In Dutch oven or shallow (2½- to 3-quart) casserole, heat bacon drippings; brown meat on all sides about 15 minutes; turn often. Add salt, Worcestershire sauce, pepper, thyme, mushrooms, and bouillon; blend.

Bring mixture to quick boil. Reduce heat. Cover tightly. Braise for 1 hour.

Drain off meat juices and measure; add enough water or bouillon to make 2 cups.

If stew is cooked in Dutch oven, transfer mixture to a buttered casserole. Add onions and potatoes; blend well. Pour meat juices over foods in casserole.

Cover casserole with pie crust; seal edges. Bake in a hot (450° F.) oven for 15 minutes, or until crust is brown.

NOTE: The stew can be cooked ahead; bake pastry before serving.

Serve at once with tomato slices marinated in French or Italian dressing.

Pastry for Single Pie Crust:

Total Time: about 10 minutes

  1¾ cups flour
  ¼   teaspoon salt
  ⅔   cup shortening

Sift flour with salt; cut in shortening as you do for any pie crust; add enough water (about 5 tablespoons) so that mixture can be formed into a ball. Roll out on floured board to a circle that will fit the top of the casserole. Cut a hole in center of pie crust to allow steam to escape. *NOTE:* If desired, use one (2-cup) recipe of biscuit mix instead of pie crust ingredients above.

Beef Shortribs Stew ★

Total Time: about 1½ hours   Serves: 4 to 6

  3 pounds beef shortribs
  2 tablespoons fat
  1 clove garlic, mashed or puréed
  ½ cup chopped onions
  ½ cup chopped green pepper
  1 can (15 ounces) Spanish style tomato sauce
  ½ cup beef bouillon or white wine
  1 teaspoon salt
  ¼ teaspoon black pepper
  ⅛ teaspoon chili powder
  1 tablespoon prepared mustard
  1 tablespoon cider vinegar

Have meatman cut shortribs into 2-inch lengths.

In Dutch oven or heavy skillet, heat fat. Add meat and brown lightly, turning frequently, 10 to 15 minutes. Remove ribs from cooker; reserve. Add garlic, onions and pepper to fat; sauté 5 minutes, stirring frequently. Add remaining ingredients in order given; mix well. Bring mixture to quick boil. Add shortribs to sauce. Reduce heat. Cover tightly. Braise over low heat until shortribs are tender, about 1 hour. Stir once or twice during cooking.

Serve on bed of hot mashed potatoes or rice.

NOTE: For a thicker gravy, mix 2 tablespoons cornstarch with ¼ cup cold water and blend into stew shortly before serving. Simmer until stew is well blended and sauce thickens.

Curried Beef en Casserole ★

Total Time: about 1¾ hours   Serves: 6 to 8

2½ to 3 pounds boneless beef (chuck or sirloin tip) cut in 1-inch cubes
3 tablespoons flour
1 teaspoon salt
3 tablespoons butter or margarine
2 cups chopped onions
1½ teaspoons curry powder
⅛ teaspoon white pepper
½ cup beef bouillon or consommé
½ cup tomato juice
½ cup white wine

In bowl or plastic bag containing a mixture of flour and salt, dredge meat, a few cubes at a time. Coat thoroughly; shake off excess flour.

In (2- to 2½-quart) casserole, heat butter. Brown meat slowly, turning frequently, about 10 minutes. Add onions, curry powder, and pepper; sauté for 5 minutes, stirring frequently. Meanwhile, blend bouillon with tomato juice and wine; pour over meat.

Cover, and bake in a slow (325° F.) oven for 1 hour. Increase to moderate (350° F.) oven and cook until meat is tender, about 20 minutes.

Serve in casserole, with hot fluffy rice and pickles in separate dishes.

BOILED BEEF

"Boiled" beef must never be boiled. The popular name is most misleading. Actually, boiled beef is simmered, with the covering water at a gentle bubble, below the boiling point of water.

Cuts to Select for Boiled Beef

The cuts for boiled beef are usually in one large piece. Some cuts contain considerable bone; others are boneless. The neck, heel of round, shortribs, ox joints, plate, and crosscut shank are available bone-in or boned.

Heel of round.

Heel of round

Short ribs.

Short ribs

Ox joints.

Ox joints

Plate.

Plate

Crosscut shanks.

Crosscut shanks

Boneless beef brisket: called "boiling beef."

Fresh brisket

Cured beef brisket: called "corned beef."

Corned brisket

How to Plan Boiled Beef Servings

ONE AVERAGE SERVING	POUNDS PER SERVING
Lean Meat with less bone	⅓–½
Fattier meat with more bone	½–¾

For step-by-step directions to refrigerate or freeze fresh and cooked boiled beef, see *Meat Storage in Transit.* See also *Carving Made Easy.*

How to Cook "Boiled Beef" ★
(Basic Recipe)

Put meat in large pot or deep kettle and cover with cold water. Add ½ teaspoon salt for each pound of meat. If desired, add a peeled onion studded with cloves.

Cover and simmer until meat is tender, usually between 3 to 4 hours. Larger cuts will need up to 5 hours.

Add fresh vegetables during the last 30 minutes of cooking.

Cured and corned meat: If very salty, soak in cold water for about ½ hour before cooking. Add no seasoning. Skim off fat and scum that rise to top when water comes to a boil.

Guide to
Simmering Time For Boiled Beef
(per pound of meat)

Fresh or corned beef	40–50 minutes
Fresh tongue	50 minutes
Smoked or cured tongue	35–40 minutes

TIME-SAVERS!! Because of the long cooking hours, cook-ahead preparation or pressure-cooking is strongly recommended.

How to Carve Beef Brisket

See *Carving Made Easy* page 240.

New England Boiled Dinner ★

Total Time: about 4 hours   Serves: 10 or more

     5 pounds corned beef brisket
     1 bay leaf
     8 peppercorns
     4 large yellow turnips, peeled and sliced
     6 large carrots, scraped and quartered
     6 parsnips, scraped and halved
    12 small peeled onions
     6 medium-sized potatoes, peeled and halved
     1 head green cabbage, cut in wedges

In large kettle, cover meat with cold water. Add bay leaf and peppercorns. Bring water to quick boil; skim off fat. Cover pot; reduce heat. Simmer over very low heat until meat is tender, about 3 to 4 hours.

During the last 45 minutes, when meat is barely tender, add the vegetables; cover and simmer until meat and vegetables are tender.

To serve: Drain meat; place in center of hot serving platter. Slice meat across the grain. Surround with drained vegetables. Serve with prepared horseradish and pickles.

Austrian-Style Boiled Beef ★

Total Time: about 4 hours   Serves: about 6

    4 pounds beef with bone (brisket, shin, plate, chuck or
       round)
    Boiling water
    2 to 3 leeks, trimmed and washed(!)
    ½ teaspoon dried thyme or basil
    2 small bay leaves, crumbled
    ⅛ teaspoon caraway seeds
    2 scraped carrots
    1 medium-sized onion, pricked with fork
    1 celery stalk with leaves
    1 white turnip, scraped and sliced
    6 (or more) peppercorns
    Salt and white pepper, to taste

In large kettle, barely cover meat with boiling water.
Bring to quick boil; skim off fat and scum. Add all ingredients except salt and white pepper. Cover lightly.
Simmer over very low heat until meat is tender, 3 to 4
hours. Season with salt and pepper.

To serve: Drain meat; place on hot platter and slice.
Serve with Quick Horseradish Sauce (see *Index*) and
jacket-boiled potatoes sprinkled with minced parsley.

NOTE: Strain cooking liquid; season to taste; serve in
small soup cups; garnish with minced parsley or chopped
chives. Save remaining soup for use in cooking; or freeze.

Pennsylvania Dutch Brisket of Beef ★

Total Time: about 2½ hours   Serves: 6 to 8

     1½ quarts sauerkraut
      2 tablespoons caraway seeds
      2 tablespoons flour
      3 to 4 pounds brisket of beef
      1 cup applesauce
      2 tablespoons brown sugar
     ½ cup chopped onions
         Boiling water

In Dutch oven or large heavy saucepan, spread one-half the sauerkraut. Sprinkle with 1 tablespoon caraway seeds mixed with flour.

Add meat; spread with a mixture of applesauce, sugar and onions. Cover with remaining sauerkraut mixed with 1 tablespoon caraway seeds.

Barely cover with boiling water. Cover tightly. Simmer over low heat until meat is tender, about 2 to 2½ hours. Serve with jacket potatoes.

GROUND BEEF

Ground beef is one of the thriftiest meats to serve as an attractive quick 'n' easy main dish. Hamburgers, or burgers as they are often called, are number one favorites with the young.

Ground beef is as easy to cook as it is to eat; and yet it is often ruined by careless preparation.

Ground beef can be broiled, baked or barbecued. It makes juicy burgers, loaves, tiny balls and hearty meat sauces for the popular pasta. It is used for countless unusual dishes all over the world.

How to Plan Ground Beef Servings

As a rule of thumb, there are four average servings in one pound. Allowing for extra helpings, 1½ to 2 pounds will yield six servings.

For step-by-step directions to refrigerate or freeze fresh and cooked ground beef, see *Meat Storage in Transit*.

How to Select Ground Beef

With a good-grade meat that is low in fat, but not without some, there is the least waste and shrinkage.

Ready-ground beef: This is often labeled as "hamburger" in meat markets. Usually it has more fat than ground-to-order beef.

Ground-to-order beef: Coarsely ground boned chuck is best in flavor; it also has the right fat content to keep burgers juicy. Boned round beef is another good choice; it has slightly less fat content, which reducers appreciate. Nonreducers may want to have bone marrow added to the meat before grinding or to brush burgers with a speck of butter before or after cooking.

Twice-ground beef: This is sometimes preferred for meat loaves and meat balls because it makes them more compact.

The Basic Hamburger

Total Time: about 20 minutes   Serves: 4

1 pound ground beef (chuck)
2 to 3 tablespoons cold liquid: tomato juice, bouillon
   or club soda
Seasonings:
   1 teaspoon salt and ⅛ teaspoon black pepper, or
   ½ teaspoon garlic or onion salt with a dash of dried
      marjoram or tarragon
   2 to 3 tablespoons finely chopped onions (optional)

Handle meat as little and as lightly as possible. Blend
liquid with seasonings before mixing with meat; flavors will
be distributed more evenly, and the meat patties will
puff up and be juicier. If onions are added, blend into
liquid first.

Shape mixture loosely into patties ¾ to 1 inch thick,
with outer edges as high as the center.

Broil hamburgers like steaks in preheated broiler. Place
patties on broiler rack. Insert rack in broiler pan which
has been lined with foil. Broil about 3 inches below source
of heat to desired doneness. Turn once with tongs or pancake turner.

Guide to
Total Broiling Time for Burgers

	MINUTES
¾-inch-thick patties	
rare	8
medium	12
well done	15
1-inch-thick patties	
rare	10
medium	14
well done	18

Panbroil on top of stove in heavy skillet or on a ridged griddle with just enough fat to keep patties from sticking. Pour off fat as it accumulates. Turn to cook evenly to desired doneness. Or panbroil hamburgers in a heated heavy skillet sprinkled with a thin, even layer of salt instead of fat.

Charcoal-broil hamburgers with care; the meat should have the fragrant taste but never the looks of charcoal.

To serve: Place hamburgers on hot platter or on soft buns, English muffins, garlic bread, pumpernickel, onion rolls—all heated, toasted or grilled.

Seasoning variations: For chopped onions in recipe, add a tablespoon prepared light mustard to meat mixture.

Favorite Hamburger "Mates"

Foods: thinly sliced raw onions sprinkled with salt and pepper; smothered onions; fried onion rings; pickles— whole, sliced or in mustard sauce; whole or sliced stuffed green or ripe olives; sliced American cheese or cheese cubes; tomatoes, either raw cut wedges or broiled halves; green pepper rings or strips in sour cream or mayonnaise; sauerkraut with caraway seeds; French fries or potato chips; cole slaw.

Sauces: catsup; chili sauce; a mixture of two parts catsup and one part prepared horseradish; barbecue sauce seasoned with lemon juice; Worcestershire or other meat sauces.

The Basic Meat Loaf ★
(Beef)

It is a mixture of ground meat and a filler, blended with beaten eggs, delicately flavored with herbs and spices and moistened with a small quantity of liquid. Ingredients are tossed lightly, at best with a two-tined fork.

The ground meat may be beef or a mixture of beef, pork

and veal. "Fillers" may be bread crumbs, bread soaked in water or milk, cooked rice, uncooked oatmeal, crushed corn flakes, wheat germ or other cereals. The moistening liquid may be water, milk, bouillon, soup stock, leftover meat juices, tomato juice or wine. Twice-ground beef makes a firmer loaf.

The easiest way to cook a loaf is to bake it. It can also be made on top of stove in a skillet with a dome cover or in an electric table cooker.

The shape of a meat loaf varies. It can be shaped with wet hands and placed in a shallow pan for a crusty loaf. For a moist loaf, it can be packed into an oiled loaf pan, a ring mold or in several muffin pans or custard cups.

A meat loaf may be topped with bacon or salt pork slices and basted occasionally during baking with tomato juice. A loose dome cover made of foil and placed over the loaf will keep the meat loaf soft and extra juicy.

A meat loaf can be served hot or cold.

Total Time: 30–60 minutes   Serves: 4 to 6

- 1 cup fresh bread crumbs
- 1 or 2 eggs, slightly beaten
- 1 teaspoon salt or garlic salt
- ⅛ teaspoon black pepper
- 1 teaspoon Worcestershire sauce or ½ teaspoon dried sage
- ½ cup milk or water
- 1 pound ground beef (chuck)

In large bowl, mix first six ingredients thoroughly. Lightly mix in meat and blend.

Shape mixture into one large or six small oval loaves; place in a shallow, lightly-oiled pan. Bake until well done.

To serve hot: Rest meat loaf on a hot platter for 15 minutes before slicing. If served cold, make thin, even slices.

To reheat cold meat loaf: Place on large square of heavy foil and brush with melted butter or oil; wrap and place in moderate (350° F.) oven for 15 minutes or until thoroughly heated.

Serve with broiled or baked tomato halves; tomato or mushroom sauce; steamed broccoli and a mixed salad with French dressing or tangy cole slaw.

Baking Time for Meat Loaves

	IN MODERATE (350° F.) OVEN	IN SLOW (325° F.) OVEN
Large loaf (as above)	45 minutes	60 minutes
6 small loaves	30 minutes	40 minutes

Meat Balls ★
(Beef)

They are usually a mixture of ground beef with one or two other meats, as in Danish and Swedish Meat Balls. They are sometimes served as an appetizer but more often with hot buttered spaghetti or macaroni and grated Italian-type cheese.

Total Time: about 25 minutes   Serves: 4 to 6

    1 cup fresh bread crumbs
    1 teaspoon salt
    ⅛ teaspoon black pepper
    1 egg, slightly beaten
    ¼ cup milk or water
    1 pound ground beef (chuck)
    2 tablespoons butter or oil
    1 teaspoon onion powder
    1 cup beef or chicken bouillon, tomato juice or red wine
    ½ cup sour cream (optional)

In large bowl, blend first five ingredients in order given. Mix thoroughly. Lightly mix in meat. Shape into 1½-inch balls.

Heat butter in heavy skillet. Brown meat balls, turning frequently, for 5 minutes. Sprinkle with onion powder. Add bouillon.

Cover and simmer for 10 to 15 minutes; shake pan occasionally. Stir sour cream into sauce; reheat if necessary. Do not boil.

NOTE: If desired, the first six ingredients may be mixed ahead of serving time and shaped into balls before cooking.

Swedish Beet-Beefburgers

Total Time: about 30 minutes   Serves: 6

    2   tablespoons butter or margarine
    ½   cup chopped onions
    1½ pounds ground beef
    2   egg yolks, slightly beaten
    1   tablespoon (or less) salt
    ⅛   teaspoon white pepper
    1   cup milk
    1   medium-sized potato, cooked or canned
    2   medium beets, cooked or canned
    2   tablespoons cider vinegar
    4   tablespoons butter or margarine

In heavy skillet, melt butter; sauté onions until golden, about 5 minutes; remove to deep bowl. Add meat, egg yolks, salt, pepper and milk.

Chop potato and beets very fine; blend with vinegar and add to meat mixture. Mix thoroughly. Shape into six round cakes about ½ inch thick.

Wipe skillet with paper towel. Heat 4 tablespoons butter. Panbroil meat cakes to a golden brown, about 5 minutes on each side for rare and 8 minutes on each side for medium doneness.

Serve at once with boiled or French fried potatoes and dilled cucumber salad.

Hamburger Special

Total Time: about 25 minutes   Serves: 6 or more

    1 can (4 ounces) mushroom stems and pieces, drained
    ½ cup minced onions
    2 tablespoons melted butter or margarine
    ½ cup fresh bread crumbs
    1 egg, beaten
    ¼ cup tomato catsup
    ½ teaspoon Worcestershire sauce
    ½ teaspoon salt
    ½ teaspoon black pepper
    2 pounds ground beef
    6 or 12 slices bacon

In large bowl, mix first nine ingredients in order given. Add meat and mix with a light hand. With wet hands, shape into six or more plump patties about 1½ inches thick. Wrap one or two slices bacon around each burger; fasten ends with toothpicks. Place meat on broiler rack. Insert rack in broiler pan which has been lined with foil. Broil 6 inches below source of heat for 10 minutes. Turn with tongs or pancake turner. Broil second side for about 10 minutes.

Serve at once with creamed spinach and tomato salad.

Pan-Broiled Spicy Burgers

Total Time: about 30 minutes   Serves: 6

Spice Bag:
    4 whole cloves
    1 small cinnamon stick
    4 cardamom seeds

    1 cup white wine
 1½ pounds ground beef
    3 English muffins, split and toasted

Make spice bag with cheesecloth. Place in saucepan with wine. Cover and simmer for 5 minutes; remove spice bag. Keep liquid hot.

Shape meat into six patties to fit the size of the muffins. Heat heavy skillet and sprinkle with coarse salt.

Pan-broil burgers slowly on both sides; turn once with tongs or pancake turner. Total broiling time: about 10 minutes for rare and 15 minutes for medium burgers.

When desired doneness has been reached, add wine and bring to quick boil. Remove from heat.

Serve at once on muffin halves with hot buttered spinach or French fried onion rings.

Pakistani Kima ★
(Sautéed Ground Beef)

Total Time: about 1 hour   Serves: 6

    3   tablespoons olive oil, butter or margarine
    1   cup chopped onions
 1½   pounds ground lean beef, chuck or bottom round
    3   medium tomatoes, peeled and chopped
    1   can (1 pound) small peas, undrained
    1   tablespoon curry powder
    2   teaspoons salt
    1   teaspoon paprika
    1   teaspoon garlic powder
   ½   teaspoon chili powder
   ¼   teaspoon black pepper
   ⅛   teaspoon cayenne pepper (optional)
       Eggplant in Sour Cream recipe
    3   to 4 cups hot steamed rice

In heavy skillet, heat oil; add onions and sauté until golden, about 10 minutes, stirring frequently. Add meat and tomatoes. Cover and braise over low heat for 15 minutes.

Add peas and the seven spices; blend well. Cover and

cook over very low heat until meat is tender, about 30 minutes. Serve at once with Eggplant in Sour Cream and steamed rice.

NOTE: If cooked ahead, reheat with ¼ to ½ cup added chicken broth, wine or water.

Eggplant in Sour Cream ★

Total Time: about 1 hour, including chilling   Serves: 6

    1 small eggplant
    3 tablespoons olive oil, butter or margarine
    ½ teaspoon garlic salt
    ¼ teaspoon white pepper
    1 cup sour cream or plain yogurt

Cut unpeeled eggplant into ½-inch cubes. In heavy skillet, melt oil; sauté eggplant until golden and soft, about 15 minutes. Stir occasionally while cooking. Set aside to cool. Blend garlic and pepper into sour cream; stir into eggplant. Chill for at least ½ hour before serving.

Danish Hakkebof
(Sautéed Beefsteaks)

Total Time: about 30 minutes   Serves: 6

    1½ pounds ground beef
        Salt and pepper to taste
    ½ cup flour (or less)
    ¼ cup butter or margarine
    2 onions, sliced paper thin

With wet hands, shape meat into six flat, round or oval patties. Sprinkle with salt and pepper; dredge generously with flour.

Melt one-half the butter in heavy skillet. Sauté patties for 10 minutes, turning once or twice, until meat is crisp and brown on the outside. Set aside on a hot platter.

Add remaining butter to skillet. Sauté onions until golden, turning frequently, about 5 minutes. Spoon onions onto top of meat patties.

Serve immediately with broiled tomatoes or steamed carrots and boiled or mashed potatoes.

Italian Polpette
(Sautéed Meat Balls)

Total Time: about 30 minutes   Serves: 6

    3 slices stale or toasted white bread
       Water
1½   pounds ground beef
    3 eggs, slightly beaten
    3 tablespoons grated Romano cheese
    1 clove garlic, minced or pureed
    1 tablespoon minced parsley
       Salt and black pepper, to taste
    6 tablespoons oil
    3 to 4 cups hot steamed rice

Soak bread in water for 5 minutes; squeeze dry and tear into small pieces.

In large bowl, mix meat, eggs, cheese, garlic and parsley. Add bread; season to taste. Blend very well. With wet hands, shape into twelve or eighteen balls.

Sauté in hot fat until golden brown, turning with tongs or pancake turner to cook evenly. Total cooking time is about 12 to 15 minutes, depending on size of meat balls.

Serve on bed of steamed rice with a mixed salad in Italian dressing.

The Famous Salisbury Steak

Total Time: about 45 minutes   Serves: 6

    3   tablespoons cold water, wine or bouillon
1½   teaspoons salt
⅛   teaspoon black pepper
    1   tablespoon grated onion
    1   egg, well beaten
1½   pounds ground beef, chuck or round
        Melted butter
        Mushroom caps (optional)
        Quick Meat Sauce recipe

Blend water, salt, pepper, onion and egg. Add meat and mix well with a light hand.

On an oiled shallow baking pan, mold meat mixture into the shape of a steak about 1¼ inches thick. Push up edges to give the looks of a steak. Brush top with melted butter.

Bake in a preheated hot (450° F.) oven for 10 minutes. Reduce to low heat (325° F.) and bake until meat is tender, about 25 minutes. Brush with butter once or twice during baking.

To serve: Slide "steak" onto hot platter with a slotted pancake turner; garnish with mushroom caps. Serve sauce in separate dish. Serve with buttered lima beans or a mixed vegetable.

Quick Meat Sauce

Total Time: about 5 minutes   Yield: about 1 cup

¼   pound butter or margarine
    1   tablespoon Worcestershire sauce
¾   cup red wine
    1   teaspoon minced parsley or chives

In small saucepan, melt butter until it begins to brown. Add Worcestershire sauce and liquid. Stir and boil for 1 minute. Sprinkle with parsley before serving.

Iranian Beef and Eggplant Casserole

Total Time: about 45 minutes   Serves: 6 or more

```
    1  large eggplant
    4  tablespoons olive or salad oil
       Salt and black pepper to taste
 1½    pounds ground beef, chuck or round
   ½   cup sliced onions
    2  cups cut-up tomatoes, fresh or canned
    1  cup seedless raisins
    1  cup pistachio or pine nuts (optional)
    3  to 4 cups hot steamed rice
       Ripe olives
```

Cut unpeeled eggplant in ½-inch slices. Heat 2 tablespoons oil in heavy skillet and sauté eggplant about 10 minutes, stirring occasionally. Remove eggplant and reserve.

Heat 2 tablespoons oil in same skillet. Brown meat and onions for 5 minutes, turning frequently. Add tomatoes, raisins and nuts. Bring mixture to boil; remove from heat.

In well-oiled (2-quart) casserole, place alternate layers of eggplant and meat mixture; make top layer meat. Bake in a moderate (350° F.) oven until all liquid is absorbed and top is browned, about 30 minutes.

Serve with steamed rice and black (ripe) olives in separate dishes.

Mid-Eastern Oven Kabobs
(Baked Hamburgers)

Total Time: about 45 minutes   Serves: 6

2 pounds lean beef, chuck or bottom round
1 large onion, chopped fine
1 tablespoon plain yogurt or sour cream
1 teaspoon salt
¼ teaspoon cloves
¼ teaspoon ground cardamom seeds
¼ teaspoon white pepper
¼ teaspoon ground cumin seeds (optional)
¼ teaspoon ginger

In deep bowl, mix ingredients in order given; blend well yet lightly. With wet hands, form mixture into 12 uniform balls. Roll balls into 4-inch-long pieces or flatten into patties 3 inches in diameter. Preheat oven to 350° F.

Place kabobs on ungreased baking sheet. Bake in a moderate (350° F.) oven for 15 minutes. Turn with pancake turner; check doneness.

Bake 10 minutes longer for rare or 15 minutes longer for medium kabobs.

Serve with hot steamed rice or kasha; and plain yogurt or sour cream in separate dishes.

Scotch Meat Loaf

Total Time: about
1¼ hours for loaf;   Serves: 6
1 hour for mold;
35 minutes for small loaves

  1½ pounds ground beef (chuck)
  ¼ pound salt pork, chopped fine
   1 cup uncooked oatmeal
  ½ cup chopped onions
  ½ cup chopped green pepper
  ¼ teaspoon black pepper
  ¼ teaspoon paprika
   1 teaspoon prepared mustard
   2 eggs, beaten
  ½ cup sherry or bouillon
  ¾ cup tomato juice

In deep bowl, mix all ingredients thoroughly with a light hand. Pack firmly into a well-greased loaf pan, mold or six small loaf pans. Bake in a moderate (375° F.) oven. Release edges with spatula to unmold. Turn on heated platter. Let large loaf rest for 5 minutes before slicing. Spoon meat juices onto top of servings.

Serve with a Chef's salad and French or Italian bread.

Approximate Baking Time

	MINUTES
Loaf	60
Mold	45
Small loaves	20

Pizza-Burger "Pie"

Total Time: about 45 minutes   Serves: 6

  1½ pounds ground beef (chuck)
  1½ teaspoons salt
  ½   teaspoon pepper
  1½ cups canned tomato sauce
  1   teaspoon dried basil
  1   small onion, finely sliced
  1   can (2 ounces) flat anchovy fillets, drained and
      chopped
  ¾   cup thinly sliced Mozzarella cheese
  2   tablespoons minced parsley

In bowl, blend beef with salt and pepper. Spread evenly in oiled and floured (8- or 9-inch) pie plate. Mix tomato sauce with basil and onion; pour over meat. Dot with anchovies and cheese.

Bake in a preheated moderate (350° F.) oven for about 25 minutes. Cut into wedges.

Sprinkle with parsley before serving. Serve with crusty bread or potato chips and a huge bowl of tossed salad greens.

Texan Chili Con Carne ★

Total Time: about 45 minutes   Serves: 4 to 6

   2 tablespoons lard or bacon drippings
   1 pound ground beef
   1 cup chopped onions
   1 cup chopped green pepper
   1 clove garlic, minced or puréed
   1 teaspoon salt
 ½ teaspoon black pepper
   1 tablespoon chili powder
   1 can (8 ounces) tomato sauce
   2 cans (1 pound each) tomatoes
   1 can (1 pound) red kidney beans, drained
   Soda crackers

In large heavy skillet, melt lard; add beef, onions, green pepper, garlic, salt and pepper; sauté for 15 minutes, stirring frequently.

Blend chili powder with tomato sauce, tomatoes and kidney beans; add to meat mixture and mix well with a light hand.

Cover and simmer over low heat until slightly thickened, about 25 minutes.

Serve piping hot with soda crackers in separate dish.

NOTE: If cooked ahead, prepare dish without chili powder. Add 1 tablespoon chili powder with 2 tablespoons boiling water when reheating.

Beef Porcupines

Total Time: about 1 hour   Serves: 6

  1 pound ground beef
  ½ cup uncooked regular long-grain white rice
  2 tablespoons minced onion or 1 tablespoon onion
     powder
  2 tablespoons chili sauce or catsup
  2 teaspoons salt
  1 teaspoon celery salt
  2 cups canned tomatoes, undrained
  2 tablespoons minced parsley

In a large bowl, mix meat with rice, onion, chili sauce, and salt. Shape into 12 balls of uniform size. *NOTE:* When the dish is finished, the grains of rice will stick out to resemble porcupine needles.

For baking, place balls in a shallow casserole. For top-of-stove braising, place in heavy skillet. Blend celery salt into tomatoes. Pour over meat balls.

Bake, covered, in a moderate (350° F.) oven or cover and braise on top of stove until rice is tender, about 45 minutes.

Sprinkle with parsley and serve with corn on the cob or buttered peas.

Königsberger Klöpse in Kapern Sosse
(German Meat Balls in Caper Sauce)

Total Time: about 1¼ hours   Serves: 4 to 6

Meat Balls:
  4 tablespoons butter or margarine
  ½ cup chopped onions
  2 slices white bread soaked in water and squeezed dry
  1 pound lean ground beef (chuck)
  1 egg, slightly beaten
  1 teaspoon salt
  ¼ teaspoon white pepper
  ¼ cup toasted dry bread crumbs

Caper Sauce:
  2 tablespoons butter or margarine
  2 tablespoons flour
  2 cups hot bouillon or consommé
  1 tablespoon capers (more to taste)
  1 teaspoon sugar
  ½ lemon, sliced paper thin
  Salt to taste

To make meat balls: Melt 2 tablespoons butter in skillet; sauté onions until soft, about 5 minutes. Tear bread into small pieces.

In large bowl, mix meat with onion, bread, egg, salt and pepper. Blend well. With wet hands, shape mixture into balls the size of an egg. Roll in toasted bread crumbs.

Melt remaining 2 tablespoons butter in skillet; brown meat balls quickly, turning frequently, about 5 minutes. Set aside.

To make sauce: Melt butter in skillet; when it sizzles, stir in flour and cook until golden brown. Gradually add hot soup and stir until smooth. Add remaining ingredients.

Cover skillet; reduce heat and simmer for 15 minutes. Add meat balls. Cover and simmer over low heat until tender, 25 to 30 minutes.

Serve immediately with sauerkraut and a spicy tomato salad.

Stuffed Cabbage Head
(A Bohemian Dish)

Total Time: about 1½ hours   Serves: 6

    1 small head red or green cabbage
    1 pound ground beef
    2 to 3 tablespoons minced parsley
    1 teaspoon salt
    ½ teaspoon black or white pepper
    ¼ teaspoon dried marjoram
    1 cup chicken broth or water

Wash and drain cabbage. Cut a 1½-inch-thick slice from top and scoop out center. (Use for scalloped cabbage.) Mix meat with parsley and the three seasonings; spoon into cabbage.

Replace cabbage slice on top; wrap in cheesecloth or tie with string.

Place cabbage in Dutch oven with rack in bottom. Add broth. Cover tightly. Simmer over low heat until tender, about 45 to 60 minutes, depending on size of cabbage.

Serve with buttered garlic bread slices.

Hungarian Beef Doves ★
(Stuffed Cabbage Leaves)

Total Time: about 1½ hours   Serves: 6 to 8

- 12 large outer leaves of large cabbage
- 1½ pounds ground beef (chuck)
- 1 cup chopped onions
- 1 tablespoon paprika
- 2 teaspoons salt
- 2 eggs, slightly beaten
- 1 can (28 ounces) tomatoes
- 1 can (8 ounces) tomato sauce
- 1 tablespoon lemon juice
- ½ to 1 cup brown sugar

Trim thick part off outer cabbage leaves. For easy rolling, drop leaves into boiling water; remove after 2 minutes and place on paper towels.

In large bowl, mix beef with onion, paprika, salt and eggs; divide mixture into twelve equal parts. Place a mound in cup part of each leaf. Loosely fold over sides of leaves. Roll up and fasten each roll with a soft string.

Place rolls seam-side down in Dutch oven with rack in bottom. Blend tomatoes with tomato sauce and lemon juice. Pour over cabbage. Sprinkle with sugar to taste. Cover tightly; simmer until leaves are tender, about 1 hour.

Serve with buttered kernel corn and cucumber salad.

Spicy Meat Sauce for Pasta Lovers ★

Total Time: about 1½ hours   Serves: 6

   2 tablespoons olive or salad oil
   ½ cup chopped onions
   1 pound ground beef
   1 clove garlic, mashed or pureed, or ⅛ teaspoon garlic
     powder
   1 tablespoon minced parsley
   1 can (15 ounces) Spanish style tomato sauce
   1 can (7 ounces) tomato paste
   1 can (4 ounces) pimientos, chopped
   ½ cup sherry or red wine
   ½ teaspoon sugar or honey
     Salt and pepper to taste
   ½ teaspoon chili powder
   1 teaspoon Worcestershire sauce
   ½ cup chopped ripe olives

In heavy skillet, heat oil; sauté onions until light brown, stirring frequently, about 10 minutes. Push onions to one side of skillet; add beef and sauté about 10 minutes, turning often. Add garlic, parsley, tomato sauce and paste, pimientos, wine, sugar, salt and pepper. Blend well.

Cover and simmer over low heat, stirring occasionally, about 45 minutes.

Add chili powder, Worcestershire sauce and olives. Add a few tablespoons water or wine, if sauce is too thick. Cover and simmer for 15 minutes.

Serve over hot spaghetti or other pasta.

LAMB

The flesh of good-quality young lamb is finely grained yet firm in texture and dull pinkish to pinkish red in color. Its chalky white hard fat is abundant and gives flavor to the lean. The bones are porous, moist, and pinkish where cut. The four-ridged "break joint" tells the lamb's age; usually between 8 to just under 12 months, sometimes younger. "Spring lamb" is now available year-round.

Mutton, the meat of fully matured sheep, is darker in color than lamb; its fat is more brittle and without the pinkish tint. Mutton meat is cherished by many, including the British and the Mid-Eastern peoples, as a great delicacy.

All lamb is naturally tender and juicy. To keep its tenderness and prevent shrinkage, always cook lamb at low temperatures to the medium, not the well-done, stage. In America, lamb is all too often overcooked and underseasoned.

Green seasonings, such as mint, basil, marjoram, parsley, rosemary, and thyme, go very well with lamb; and so do green side-dish vegetables, such as asparagus, beans and lima beans, broccoli, young onions, tender green peas, pepper, and spinach. See *Flavors to Flatter*.

No matter how lamb is cooked, always serve it either piping hot or very well chilled; never lukewarm!

For step-by-step directions to refrigerate and freeze fresh and cooked lamb, see *Meat Storage in Transit*. See also *Carving Made Easy*.

How to Select Lamb Cuts

All thriftier cuts can be prepared in at least two different ways. Compare prices and select accordingly.

SHOULDER CUTS

Bone-in square: much bone; hard to carve. Roast or pot-roast.

Square shoulder

Cushion: boned to form pocket for stuffing; tied to keep shape. Roast or pot-roast.

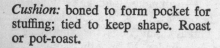
Cushion shoulder

Boned and rolled roast: tender, juicy meat; easy to carve. Roast or pot-roast.

Rolled shoulder

Arm chops: with round bone. Broil, pan-broil, or braise.

Arm chop

Blade chops: with considerable bone. Broil, pan-broil, or braise.

Blade chop

Saratoga chops: boneless. Broil, pan-broil, or braise.

Saratoga chops

Cubed lamb for stews: Braise.

Cubed lamb for kabobs: Broil.

Cubes for kabobs

BREAST CUTS

Bone-in: Roast or pot-roast.

Boned: with pocket for stuffing: Roast or pot-roast.

Breast

Boned and rolled: Roast or pot-roast.

Rolled breast

Cubed lamb for stews: Braise.

Cubed lamb for kabobs: Broil.

Cubed lamb

Riblets: Braise, barbecue, or broil.

Riblets

Neck cuts: sliced; with neck bones (a ¾-inch slice = about ½ pound). Braise.

Neck slices

Shank: available whole or cut (1 to 2 pounds each). Cook whole shank as pot roast. Cook cut shank (for stew) by braising.

Fore shank

Ground meat: often a mixture of breast, neck, flank, shank, and shoulder. For loaves, bake the ground meat. For patties, broil.

Hind shank

How to Plan Lamb Servings

Since much depends on how you cook a selected cut, it is difficult to figure average servings. Here are some guidelines.

		ONE AVERAGE SERVING
OVEN ROASTS		
Shoulder	bone-in meat	½–¾ lb.
	boned meat	¼–½ lb.
POT ROASTS		
Shoulder	bone-in meat	½–¾ lb.
	boned meat	¼–½ lb.
Breast	bone-in meat	¾–1 lb.
	boned and rolled	⅔ lb.
Shank	(weight: 1–2 pounds)	1 shank
STEWS		
Shoulder	bone-in meat	½–¾ lb.
	boned meat, 2-inch cubes	⅓–½ lb.
Breast	cut in 2-rib pieces	¾–1 lb.
Neck slices	(about ¾ inch thick)	¾–1 lb.
Shank		1 shank
CHOPS (Shoulder)	braised (¾ to 1 inch thick)	1 chop
	broiled (1 to 2 inches thick)	1 chop
	panbroiled or fried (½ to ¾ inch thick)	1 chop
BROILED MEATS		
Kabobs	boned shoulder	⅓–¾ lb.
Neck Slices	broiled or braised (about ¾ inch thick)	2 slices
RIBLETS		3 riblets
PATTIES OR LOAVES		¼–⅓ lb.

Five Ways to Cook the Thrift Cuts of Lamb

Roasting (Baking) for all shoulder cuts; boned and rolled breast; ground-meat loaves.

Trim excess fat from meat. Leave the fell on. Season. Place fat side up on rack in open shallow roasting pan. Insert meat thermometer. Add no water. Do not cover. Do not baste. Roast in a preheated slow (300° F. to 325° F.) oven to desired degree of doneness or an internal meat temperature of 175° F. to 180° F. Remove fell for easier carving. Remove fat from meat juices; see shortcut on page 252. Serve roast on preheated platter.

Roasting Time for Lamb

	PER POUND
Bone-in and cushion shoulder; stuffed and rolled breast; boned and rolled shoulder loaves	30–35 minutes 40–45 minutes

Braising for roasts, chops and stews.

Trim excess fat from meat. Brown slowly on all sides. Spoon or drain off excess fat after browning. Season. Add a small amount of liquid: ½ to ¾ cup, depending on recipe. Cover cooker tightly. Braise until tender. Remove fat from meat juices if necessary. Total braising time varies with the amount of bone and fat in a cut.

Guide to
Braising Time for Lamb
(After Browning)

Shoulder pot roast, boned and rolled:
2–3 pounds	1½–2 hours
3–4 pounds	2 hours
4–5 pounds	2¼–2½ hours

Shoulder chops:
½–¾ inch thick	35–40 minutes
¾–1¼ inches thick	45–60 minutes

Breast:
stuffed, 2–3 pounds	1½–2 hours
boned and rolled, 1½–2 pounds	1½–2 hours

Neck: slices, ¾ inch thick	1–1¼ hours
Riblets	1½–2½ hours
Shanks: about ¾–1 pound each	1–1½ hours
Stew: shoulder or breast in 1½-inch cubes	1½–2 hours

Broiling (Grilling) for chops 1 to 2 inches thick; and ground patties.

Remove fell and excess fat from chops. Slash fat edge, if necessary. Marinate if desired. Preheat broiler. Place meat on rack of broiler pan lined with foil. Broil 3 to 5 inches below source of heat until browned. Turn with tongs or slotted pancake turner. Broil second side. Season after broiling. Serve at once on hot platter.

Guide to Broiling Time for Lamb

	TOTAL TIME (IN MINUTES)
Shoulder chops	
1 inch thick	10–12
1½ inches thick	18
2 inches thick	22
Riblets, 1 inch thick	20
Ground Patties	
1 inch thick	15–18
¾ inch thick	14–15

To test doneness: cut a slit in chops and note inside color. Pinkish is medium; gray is well done.

Pan-Broiling for ½ to ¾-inch-thick chops and patties. Preheat heavy skillet or griddle. Brown meat slowly on both sides. Add no fat or water. Do not cover. Turn often to cook evenly. Pour off fat as it accumulates. Season. Serve at once.

Total broiling time is about one-half that of boiling; see above.

Pressure-Cooking for pot roasts and stews; not recommended for chops.

Irish Roast Shoulder of Lamb

Total Time: Serves: 8 or more
for a 4-pound roast, about 3 hours

    1 boned and rolled lamb shoulder, about 4 pounds
    ½ teaspoon salt
    ½ teaspoon dry mustard
    ½ teaspoon dried rosemary
    Currant-Mint Sauce recipe

Rub lamb with a mixture of salt, mustard and rosemary. Place on rack in shallow open roasting pan. Insert meat thermometer. Roast in a slow (325° F.) oven until meat thermometer registers 175° F. to 180° F. Allow 40 to 45 minutes per pound of meat for roasting. Defat pan juices if necessary; serve in separate dish.

Serve roast on preheated platter with steamed spinach and potatoes; and Currant Mint sauce.

Currant-Mint Sauce

Total Time: about 5 minutes   Yield: about 2 cups

Shortly before roast is done, blend 1 cup each of currant and mint jelly with fork; add 2 tablespoons lime or orange juice and ½ cup minced fresh mint leaves. Blend well.

Italian Lamb Roast

Total Time: 2½ to 3 hours   Serves: 6 or more

        3 to 4 pounds rolled and boned lamb shoulder
        1 teaspoon salt
        ⅛ teaspoon white pepper
        4 cloves garlic, mashed or puréed
        ½ teaspoon dried rosemary
        ¼ teaspoon grated lemon rind
        1 tablespoon melted butter or margarine
        ¼ cup olive oil
        1 cup dry white wine

Rub meat with a mixture of salt, pepper, garlic, rosemary and lemon rind. Place meat on rack in open roasting pan; insert meat thermometer.

Roast in a preheated slow (325° F.) oven for 40 to 45 minutes per pound of meat, until thermometer registers

170° F. for rare
175° F. for medium rare
180° F. for a well-done roast.

Baste roast frequently with a mixture of melted butter and olive oil; alternate basting with wine.

When desired degree of doneness has been reached, remove roast to preheated platter; keep hot.

Skim fat off meat juices in roasting pan. Reheat if necessary; check and correct seasoning with additional salt and pepper. Serve sauce in separate dish without thickening. Serve with creamed spinach or buttered broccoli and steamed rice.

Roast Lamb Shanks—French Style ★

Total Time: Serves: 4
to marinate, 2 hours or overnight
to roast, about 1 hour

4 lamb shanks totaling about 4 pounds, well trimmed of
    fat

Marinade:
1½ cups red wine or Burgundy
 2 teaspoons salt
½ teaspoon black pepper
 1 clove garlic, mashed or puréed
 1 bay leaf

Steamed spinach

Place meat in a deep bowl; cover with marinade. Cover and marinate at room temperature for 2 hours or in the refrigerator overnight. Baste occasionally. Drain meat; reserve marinade.

Place meat on rack in shallow roasting pan; brush with marinade.

Roast in preheated hot (400° F.) oven for 15 minutes. Baste. Reduce to moderate (350° F.) heat and roast until shanks are tender, about 45 minutes. Baste frequently with marinade. Skim fat from pan juices and reheat with remaining marinade. Serve shanks on bed of steamed spinach; pour marinade over meat.

Hungarian Lamb Shanks ★

Total Time: about 2 hours   Serves: 4 or more

    4 lamb shanks, cut in serving pieces
    1 teaspoon salt
    1 tablespoon Hungarian paprika
    3 to 4 tablespoons fat
    1 teaspoon salt
  ¼ teaspoon dried oregano
    Hot water
    8 small potatoes, scraped (not peeled)
    8 small onions, pricked with fork
    4 medium carrots, cut in halves
    1 pound cut green beans

Rub lamb pieces with a mixture of salt and paprika. In Dutch oven or heavy skillet, heat fat; sauté meat and brown, turning frequently, for 10 minutes. Add salt and oregano and enough hot water to barely cover meat.

Cover tightly. Braise over low heat for 45 minutes.

Add potatoes, onions and carrots. Cover and braise for 30 minutes. Do not add water.

Add beans, Cover and braise for 15 minutes or until meat and vegetables are tender. Check seasoning; if necessary, season with salt and black pepper to taste.

Serve piping hot with steamed corn on the cob or a tossed green salad.

Mexican Lamb Shanks ★

Total Time: about 2 hours   Serves: 6

   6 lamb shanks
   Flour
   2 cups chicken bouillon or water
   1 small onion, sliced
   1 bay leaf, crushed
   2 teaspoons salt
  ¼ teaspoon chili powder
  ⅛ teaspoon (more to taste) cocoa
  ⅛ teaspoon cinnamon
   1 can (15 ounces) Spanish-style tomato sauce
   1 can (4 ounces) pimientos, cut up
   Worcestershire sauce to taste

Dust shanks with flour. Place in Dutch oven or heavy skillet. Add remaining ingredients except Worcestershire sauce; blend. Cover tightly.

Braise over low heat until meat is tender, about 1½ to 2 hours.

Season to taste with Worcestershire sauce. Serve piping hot with buttered rice and pickles.

Asadito ★

("Little Lamb Roasts")

Total Time: about 1¾ hours   Serves: 4 or more

4 pounds lamb riblets
Flour
3 tablespoons bacon drippings or fat from meat
1 can (15 ounces) Spanish-style tomatoes
½ cup chopped green pepper
1½ teaspoons salt
¼ teaspoon Spanish paprika
⅛ teaspoon white pepper
About 1 cup hot chicken bouillon
½ teaspoon lemon juice
Chopped parsley or mint

Cut meat in serving pieces; dredge generously with flour.
In heavy skillet, heat fat; brown meat on all sides, about
10 minutes. Pour off excess fat.

Add tomatoes, green pepper, the three seasonings and
enough bouillon to keep meat moist; blend well. Cover
tightly.

Braise over low heat until meat is tender, about 1½
hours. Actual cooking time will depend on the size of the
riblets.

Add lemon juice and blend. Sprinkle generously with
parsley. Serve piping hot with steamed corn on the cob or
Spanish rice.

Stuffed Lamb Breast ★
(A Pot Roast)

Total Time: about 2 hours   Serves: 4 or more
    1 large lamb breast, about 3 pounds
    Salt and pepper

Stuffing:
    3 cups soft bread crumbs
    ½ cup diced celery
    2 tablespoons chopped onions
    2 canned pimientos, chopped
    ½ teaspoon poultry seasoning
    3 tablespoons melted butter or margarine

    3 tablespoons bacon fat or oil
    ¾ cup chicken bouillon or tomato juice
    ½ cup chopped fresh mint

Have pocket cut into lamb breast from large end. Sprinkle inside and out with salt and pepper.

Pack stuffing loosely into pocket; fasten with skewers or tie securely. *NOTE:* Use packaged bread stuffing, if you wish; follow package directions.

In Dutch oven or heavy skillet, heat bacon fat; brown breast on all sides about 10 minutes. Add bouillon. Cover tightly and braise over low heat for 1 hour. Add mint. Cover and braise until meat is tender, about ½ hour.

Serve with buttered carrots and fluffy mashed potatoes. If cooked ahead, add mint when reheating the meat.

Turkish Shish Kabobs ★

Total Time: Serves: about 6
to marinate, 4–6 hours or overnight;
to prepare, about 30 minutes

2 pounds lean boned lamb shoulder, cut in 1-inch cubes

Marinade:
½ cup tarragon vinegar
½ cup sherry or red wine
2 tablespoons oil
1 clove garlic, mashed or puréed
1 teaspoon dried oregano
6 whole cloves
1 bay leaf, crushed
⅛ teaspoon salt
⅛ teaspoon black pepper

1 green pepper, cut into 6 (1½-inch) squares
6 small white onions, peeled
6 large mushroom caps
3 firm tomatoes, cut in halves

Place meat in deep bowl; cover with marinade; add the four vegetables. Blend lightly; cover and marinate in refrigerator for 4 to 6 hours or overnight. Turn occasionally.

In time for serving, set oven regulator for broiling. Preheat broiler for 10 minutes. Drain meat and vegetables. Heat marinade.

Thread on six (12 to 15-inch) metal skewers alternating pieces of lamb, onion, mushroom and tomato. Brush kabobs with marinade.

Place kabobs on oiled broiler rack. Insert rack in broiler pan lined with foil.

Broil 3 to 5 inches below source of heat until meat is tender, about 15 to 18 minutes; turn every 3 minutes and baste each time with marinade.

To serve: Rest end of each skewer on a serving plate; with a knife, push food off skewer. If desired, baste with remaining marinade. Serve with steamed brown rice or Pilaf; see *Index* for recipe.

NOTE: If you wish, place marinated lamb and vegetables in a heat-proof pan; mix with marinade and broil for 12 to 15 minutes, basting and turning every 5 minutes.

Oriental Lamb Kabobs ★

Total Time: Serves: about 6
to marinate, overnight;
to prepare, about 30 minutes

  2 pounds boned lamb shoulder, cut in 1½-inch cubes

Marinade:
  ¼ cup lemon juice
  ¼ cup wine or cider vinegar
  ¼ cup olive oil
  2 tablespoons grated onion
  1 clove garlic, mashed or puréed
  1 tablespoon ginger
  1 teaspoon salt
Optional:
  ½ teaspoon coriander seeds
  1 teaspoon turmeric

  3 firm medium tomatoes, quartered
12 onion slices, ¼ inch thick
12 green pepper strips, ½ inch thick
12 mushroom caps
Armenian Salad recipe

Trim excess fat from meat; place in bowl; cover with marinade and blend. Cover bowl and refrigerate overnight.

In time for serving, set oven regulator for broiling. Preheat broiler for 10 minutes. Drain meat. Heat marinade.

Thread on six (12 to 15-inch) metal skewers pieces of lamb, tomato, lamb, onion, lamb, green pepper, lamb, mushroom and lamb. Brush kabobs with marinade.

Place kabobs on oiled broiler rack. Insert rack in broiler pan lined with foil.

Broil 3 to 5 inches below source of heat until tender,

about 15 to 18 minutes; turn kabobs every 3 minutes and baste each time with marinade.

Serve at once with Armenian Salad and (unsalted!) steamed rice.

NOTE: If you wish, place marinated lamb and vegetables in broiler pan, blend with marinade and broil for 12 to 15 minutes, basting and turning every 5 minutes.

Aghtzen Haigagen (Armenian Salad) ★

Total Time: to prepare, about 25 minutes;   Serves: 6
to chill, 30 minutes

    16 red radishes, sliced unpeeled
     1 celery stalk, chopped
     3 medium cucumbers, scored, sliced unpeeled
    ¼ cup coarsely chopped walnuts or 3 tablespoons pistachio nuts
    ¼ cup cider vinegar
    ¼ cup olive or salad oil
     2 tablespoons lemon juice
     2 teaspoons salt
    16 ripe olives
    16 stuffed green olives

In bowl, blend vegetables and nuts; combine vinegar, oil, lemon juice and salt; pour over vegetables and toss until well coated. Garnish with olives. Chill ½ hour before serving.

Blond Irish Stew ★

This dish proves the old Irish saying, "The nearer the bone, the sweeter the meat!"

Total Time: about 1½ hours   Serves: 4 or more

2 to 3 pounds lean lamb neck, cut in 1½-inch pieces
1 cup chopped onions
Flour
3 tablespoons butter or bacon drippings
1 teaspoon salt
⅛ teaspoon white pepper
2 cloves garlic, minced or puréed
¼ teaspoon dried thyme
1 small bunch fresh parsley, tied with string
1 cup chicken bouillon or water
1 can (4 ounces) mushroom stems and pieces, undrained (optional)
½ cup evaporated milk

In paper bag or bowl, dredge meat and onions lightly with flour; shake off excess flour.

In heavy skillet, heat butter and sauté meat-onion mixture for 10 minutes; toss frequently to avoid browning. Add the five seasonings and bouillon.

Cover tightly. Braise over low heat until meat is tender, about 1 hour. Remove tied parsley. Add mushrooms and milk; blend well and reheat if necessary.

Serve piping hot with minted carrots and peas and boiled new potatoes in separate dishes. *NOTE:* If you cooked ahead, add mushrooms and milk after reheating.

Spicy Brown Lamb Stew ★

Total Time: about 2 hours   Serves: 6

```
12  lamb neck slices, ¾ inch thick
    Flour
 3  tablespoons butter or margarine
 1  cup chopped onions
 2  canned pimientos, chopped
 1  tablespoon salt
 1  clove garlic, mashed or pureed, or ⅛ teaspoon garlic
    powder
½  teaspoon ginger
¾  cup red wine or chicken bouillon
 1  can (8 ounces) tomato sauce
 2  tablespoons cornstarch (optional)
½  cup cold water or chicken bouillon (optional)
```

Dredge meat lightly with flour; shake off excess.

In Dutch oven or heavy skillet, heat fat. Brown meat on all sides, about 15 minutes; turn frequently with tongs. Pour off excess fat.

Sprinkle meat with onion, pimiento, salt, garlic and ginger. Mix wine with tomato sauce and pour over meat. Blend well.

Cover tightly. Braise over low heat until meat is tender, about 1½ hours.

For a thickened gravy, blend cornstarch with water; add to stew. Cook, stirring constantly, until gravy thickens.

Serve piping hot with buttered carrots and peas and fluffy mashed potatoes. *NOTE:* If you cooked ahead, thicken gravy after reheating.

Iranian Lamb Stew ★

Total Time: about 2 hours   Serves: 4 to 6

  2 pounds boned lamb shoulder, cut in 2-inch pieces
  3 tablespoons olive or salad oil
½ cup chopped onions
  1 teaspoon salt
¼ teaspoon dried thyme or oregano
  1 tablespoon flour
    About 2 cups boiling water
    3-inch cinnamon stick
12 dried pitted prunes, presoaked
½ teaspoon grated orange peel
    Salt and white pepper to taste
  6 baked potatoes
    Melted butter
    Chopped dill or chives

Trim excess fat from meat.

In heavy skillet, heat oil; add meat and brown, turning frequently, for 10 minutes. Add onions and sauté until golden, about 10 minutes. Remove from heat; blend in salt and thyme. Return to heat.

Blend in flour, stirring thoroughly. Gradually add enough water to moisten meat, stirring constantly. Add cinnamon stick.

Cover tightly. Braise over low heat for 1½ hours. Remove cinnamon. Add prunes and orange peel.

Cover and simmer for 20 minutes. Season to taste with salt and pepper; serve piping hot.

Rub skin of baked potatoes with butter; cut slits and add melted butter blended with dill.

NOTE: If you cook ahead, add prunes when reheating.

Caribbean Lamb–Cucumber Stew ★

Total Time: about 2 hours   Serves: 4 to 6

    3 pounds lamb stew meat
    1 teaspoon salt
    ½ teaspoon dried rosemary
    ¼ teaspoon black pepper
    ¼ cup oil
    1 cup chopped onions
    2 stalks celery, chopped fine
    1 green pepper, thinly sliced
    ½ sweet red pepper, thinly sliced (optional)
    2 cloves garlic, mashed or puréed
    1½ cups hot chicken bouillon or water
    3 medium cucumbers, scored and thinly sliced
    Tomato wedges

Remove excess fat from lamb; also gristle, if any. Sprinkle with a mixture of salt, rosemary and pepper.

In Dutch oven or heavy skillet, heat oil; brown meat on all sides, about 10 minutes. Remove meat and set aside.

Remove fat in excess of 3 tablespoons from pan; add onions, celery and peppers. Sauté, stirring constantly, until onions are glazy, about 5 minutes.

Return meat; add garlic and hot bouillon; blend well.

Cover tightly and braise over low heat until meat is tender, about 1½ hours. If necessary, add a few tablespoons water after 1 hour's cooking.

Before serving, add cucumber; blend and reheat. Garnish with tomato wedges. Serve with corn bread and a tossed green salad. *NOTE:* If you cook ahead, add cucumbers after reheating.

Indian Lamb Curry ★

Total Time: about 2 hours   Serves: about 6

    2 pounds lean boned lamb shoulder, cut in 1½-inch
      cubes
    ½ cup oil
    1 medium onion, sliced
    3 cloves garlic, mashed or puréed
    1 teaspoon ginger
    2 bay leaves, crushed
    6 whole cloves
    6 whole peppercorns
    1-inch cinnamon stick
    2 firm tomatoes, quartered or chopped
    2 tablespoons curry powder
    ¼ teaspoon turmeric (optional)
    ½ tablespoon Hungarian paprika
    ½ cup dry white wine or water
    Broiled Bananas recipe

Remove excess fat from lamb; set aside. Heat oil in
heavy skillet; sauté onion until lightly browned, stirring
constantly, about 5 minutes. Add garlic, ginger, bay leaves,
cloves, peppercorns, cinnamon stick and tomatoes. Sauté
for 5 minutes, stirring constantly. Remove cinnamon.

Mix curry powder with turmeric and paprika; add wine
to make a thick paste; add to onion mixture and blend well.

Add the meat; sauté for 2 minutes, stirring constantly.
Cover tightly and braise over very low heat until meat is
tender, about 1½ hours. Add no liquid, as enough juice
forms during cooking.

Serve with Broiled Bananas and steamed rice or un-
leavened bread. For curry accompaniments, see *Pork
Curry*.

Broiled Bananas

Total Time: about 10 minutes   Serves: 6

6 ripe bananas, peeled
Lemon juice
6 bacon strips

Sprinkle bananas with lemon juice. Wrap each banana with a strip of bacon; fasten with toothpicks. Broil 3 to 5 inches below source of heat for 6 to 7 minutes, turning once. Serve at once.

Djuvece
(Yugoslavian Lamb Casserole)

Total Time: about 1¾ hours   Serves: 4 to 6

2 tablespoons lard or oil
2 cups chopped onions
3 pounds lamb stew meat or 2 pounds lean boned shoulder, cut in 2-inch pieces
2 cups stewed tomatoes
1 cup chopped green peppers
1 cup regular rice, washed and drained
1½ cups tomato juice (or slightly more)
1 teaspoon salt
¼ teaspoon black pepper
⅛ teaspoon paprika
½ cup grated Italian-type cheese

In heavy skillet, heat lard; sauté onions until glazed, about 5 minutes; stir frequently; remove and reserve.

In same skillet, sauté meat about 15 minutes; turn frequently.

In an oiled (3-quart) casserole, arrange alternate layers

of one-half the onions, meat and tomatoes; add green peppers and rice; repeat layers with remaining onions, meat and tomatoes.

Blend tomato juice with the three seasonings and pour over food in casserole. Bake, covered, in a moderate (350° F.) oven for 30 minutes. Uncover and baste with juices in casserole or with ½ cup tomato juice, if necessary. Cover and bake until meat and rice are tender, about 30 minutes.

Sprinkle with grated cheese; bake, uncovered, until cheese has browned, about 10 minutes.

Serve piping hot with a tossed green or cucumber salad with sour cream dressing.

Greek Lamb Casserole

Total Time: about 1 hour   Serves: 4 to 6

- ¼ cup olive or salad oil
- ½ clove garlic, mashed or puréed
- 1 cup chopped onions
- 1½ pounds ground lamb
- 1½ teaspoons salt
- ⅛ teaspoon white pepper
- 1 cup fresh or canned white grapes
- ¼ cup chopped ripe olives
- 2 cups sliced cooked potatoes
- 1 can (8 ounces) tomato sauce
- ½ cup red wine or grape juice
- 2-inch cinnamon stick
- 2 bay leaves
- Thin lemon slices

In heavy skillet, heat oil; add garlic and onion; sauté for 5 minutes, stirring frequently. Add meat, salt and pepper; sauté, stirring frequently, until meat is browned, about 10 minutes. Add grapes and olives; blend well.

In (1½- or 2-quart) casserole, place alternate layers of potato and meat mixture; start and end with potato layer.

Blend tomato sauce with wine and pour over food in casserole. Place cinnamon and bay leaves on top. Cover.

Bake in a moderate (350° F.) oven for 45 minutes. Remove cinnamon and bay leaves. Garnish with lemon slices. Serve with steamed leaf spinach and a tossed green salad with plain yogurt or sour cream dressing.

Lamb-and-Egg Roulade

Total Time: about 1 hour   Serves: 4 to 6

- 1½ pounds lean ground lamb
- ½ cup finely chopped onions
- ½ teaspoon salt
- ½ teaspoon garlic salt
- 6 hard-cooked eggs, coarsely chopped
- ½ cup plain yogurt
- 1 teaspoon prepared mustard
- Olive oil
- Turkish Pilaf recipe

In bowl, blend meat, onions, salt and garlic salt. With wet hands, pat mixture into rectangular shape about 7×5 inches on a sheet of waxed paper.

Mix eggs with yogurt and mustard; spread mixture on meat. Roll in jelly roll fashion; close firmly around edges.

With wide spatula or pancake turner, place meat roll carefully on oiled jelly roll pan. Brush with oil. Bake in a moderate (350° F.) oven until well done and browned, about 35 to 40 minutes.

Serve with Turkish Pilaf and tomato salad or Eggplant in Sour Cream; see *Index* for recipe.

Turkish Pilaf

Total Time: about 30 minutes   Serves: 4 to 6

Sauté 1 cup regular long-grain rice in 4 tablespoons

butter or oil, stirring until rice is evenly browned. Carefully add 2 cups consommé or bouillon; bring to quick boil. Cover tightly.

Reduce heat; simmer until rice is tender, about 20 minutes. Season with salt to taste, if desired.

NOTE: Pilaf is usually served unsalted, because Oriental dishes are quite spicy.

PORK

Fresh pork of fine quality has a firm, fine-grained, and tender lean that is free from excessive moisture; its color ranges from nearly white pink to a delicate rose. Its fat—abundant both outside and throughout the lean—is medium soft and snowy white. The cut edges of bones are porous and pinkish. Meat of older animals is less tender, darker red, and coarser in texture, with flabby fat and hard, white bones. The quality of cured and smoked pork is known by reliable brand names.

NOTE: For your greater convenience in planning meals and cooking, this book divides the great variety of pork dishes into three separate parts. *The Story of Fresh and Cured (Smoked) Pork* starts on the following page. *The Story of Ham* starts on page 141. And recipes for sausage dishes are found on page 176-180.

THE STORY OF
FRESH AND CURED (SMOKED) PORK

Pork is one of the most important less expensive meats in our bill of fare. Its protein has the same good quality as any red meat, and pork has no more calories in its lean than beef and lamb.

Only about one third of all the pork in the United

States comes to market fresh. The rest is processed: cured (pickled); cured and smoked (hams, picnics, and bacon); made into "products," such as lard, sausage, and ready-to-eat meats; salted; and canned.

Pork is perhaps the most varied, the most versatile, meat. Unlike other meats, many cuts are sold in two forms: processed (smoked or cured) and fresh. In addition, many cuts are available in three ways: with bone in, boned, and boned and rolled. While such abundant variety is most desirable in meal planning, it is sometimes confusing and oftentimes makes it hard for the homemaker to make her best economical selection. Her best yardstick is to compare prices.

Besides, the price of fresh pork varies with the seasons. During the colder months from November to March, when supply is abundant, prices usually go down.

It is for these reasons that all pork cuts are listed in the following illustrated *Pork-Buying Guide* and also in your marketing guide *How to Select Fresh and Cured (Smoked) Pork*.

Year-round economical buys include all shoulder cuts (Boston Butt, Picnic and Cushion-style, and steaks), blade and hip end of loin roasts and steaks, hocks and the shank end of ham.

Freezer space permitting, you may want to buy one larger pork cut, when on sale at attractive cost, and divide it into several parts. Use one part now, and freeze the remaining parts for use at a later time. Here are three examples.

From a *whole fresh pork shoulder* (Boston Butt) weighing between 5 and 7 pounds, you can serve three different meals: (1) a roast with the bone in; (2) two or three boneless steaks, each about ½ inch thick, to be braised, and (3) the small end of the shoulder cut, cubed and served as a stew.

From the *shank half of ham* you can serve four different meals: (1) the shank end as a boiled dinner, simmered with vegetables; then, dividing the center part into two portions, (2) bake the part with the bone in; (3) use

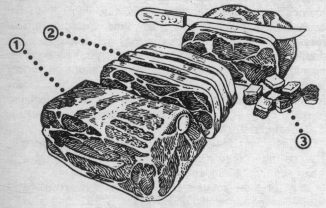

Whole fresh pork shoulder

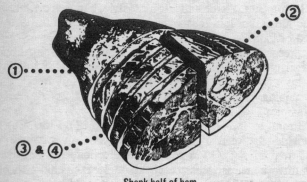

Shank-half of ham

part of the remaining half for panfried or broiled ham and (4) cube the rest and serve in a casserole dish.

From a *pork loin roast*, you can serve three different meals: (1) Have your meatman saw through the ribs high enough to leave an inch-thick layer of meat on the backbones, and chop into serving pieces. Cook like spareribs. (2) Slice several chops from the remaining piece by cutting between ribs. After the backbone has been removed, it is easy to cut these slices. Consult *Index* for recipes to serve. (3) Roast the remaining piece; see *Index* for recipes.

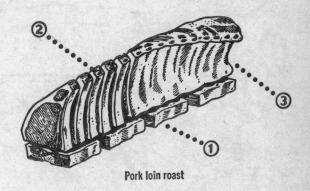

Pork loin roast

How to Select Fresh and Cured (Smoked) Pork

Always compare cost before you select the kind of pork and the cut to suit your taste.

To roast (bake): Loin (bone-in or boneless), tenderloin (whole), fresh ham (leg) (see *The Story of Ham*); shoulder butt (called Boston Butt; fresh and smoked; bone-in or boned and rolled); picnic, sometimes called Calas or

PORK BUYING GUIDE

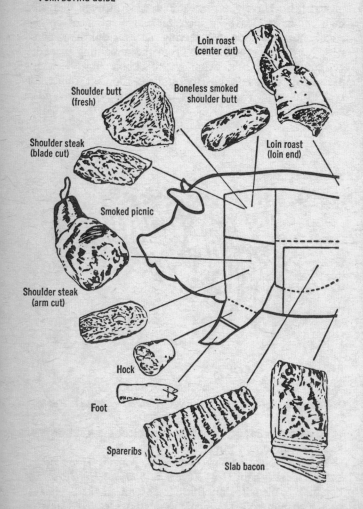

Loin roast
(center cut)

Shoulder butt
(fresh)

Boneless smoked
shoulder butt

Shoulder steak
(blade cut)

Loin roast
(loin end)

Smoked picnic

Shoulder steak
(arm cut)

Hock

Foot

Spareribs

Slab bacon

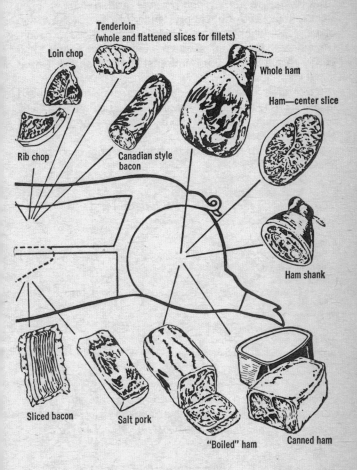

Loin chop

Tenderloin
(whole and flattened slices for fillets)

Whole ham

Ham—center slice

Rib chop

Canadian style
bacon

Ham shank

Sliced bacon

Salt pork

"Boiled" ham

Canned ham

American Meat Institute
Chicago, Ill.

Calis, fresh and smoked; arm roast and steak; Canadian-style bacon; ground-meat loaves and thick chops.

To broil, pan-broil, pan-fry and grill outdoors: Ham steaks, loin, and rib chops, tenderloin fillets, arm and blade (shoulder) steaks, shoulder roll (sliced), bacon, Canadian-style bacon, sausage (link, country-style, and patties), salt pork. For outdoors: spareribs and (marinated) kabobs.

To braise: Chops, shoulder roasts and steaks, cubed meat (stews), tenderloin (whole), spareribs and porklets.

To simmer (smoked): Ham, picnics, shoulder butt (boneless), hocks, shank.

To simmer (fresh): Shoulder butt, spareribs, backbones, hocks, pig's feet.

How to Plan Pork Servings

Cut	One Average Serving
Roasts	
bone-in meat	½–¾ lb.
boneless meat	⅓–½ lb.
Chops	
bone-in meat	½–¾ lb.
boneless meat	⅓–½ lb.
Bony cuts	
spareribs, backribs, hocks, etc.	¾–1 lb.
Ground meat and boneless stew	¼–⅓ lb.

For step-by-step directions to refrigerate and freeze fresh and smoked pork and their cooked dishes, see *Meat Storage in Transit.* See also *Carving Made Easy.*

Always Important!

For full flavor, tenderness, safety and thrift: Cook all fresh pork *slowly* until it is *well done.*

When roasting, use a meat thermometer. It is important for pork to reach the required internal temperature. See *Roasting Time for Pork*. Without a thermometer, make this eye test: cut small incisions into meat next to bone; when the meat color has changed from pink to a grayish white and the meat juices are clear (not cloudy), the meat is usually thoroughly cooked.

Before cooking, trim off excess fat.

After cooking, remove excess fat from meat juices.

Season well and with care.

Save and refrigerate all fat drippings; they find many good uses in the gourmet kitchen.

Six Ways to Cook Pork

Roasting (Baking) for cuts no less than 3 pounds. Always note oven-ready weight of meat to figure roasting time. For rib roasts, have backbone sawed free from rib and other bones before roasting; it makes carving easier.

Season meat. Place fat side up on rack in open roasting pan. Insert meat thermometer in thickest and meatiest part of pork. Add no water. Do not cover. Do not baste. Roast in a slow (325° F.) oven until well done and meat thermometer has reached desired temperature; see chart below.

Remove roast from oven. Squeeze the juice of one-half lemon over fresh pork. Rest roast 15 minutes for easier carving. Defat meat juices in roasting pan. Make gravy with milk, flour or cornstarch, if desired.

NOTE: Fresh pork roasts are excellent for rotisserie cooking in usually about one third less time than is required for oven roasting.

Roasting Time for Pork
(Oven Temperature 325° F.)

CUT	APPROXIMATE WEIGHT (POUNDS)	INTERNAL TEMPERATURE READING (DEGREES F.)	APPROXIMATE COOKING TIME (MINUTES PER POUND)
FRESH			
Leg (fresh ham)			
Whole, bone-in	12–16	170	22–26
Whole, rolled	10–14	170	24–28
Half, bone-in	5–8	170	35–40
Loin			
Center	3–5	170	30–35
Half	5–7	170	35–40
Blade loin or sirloin	3–4	170	40–45
Rolled	3–5	170	35–45
Picnic shoulder			
Bone-in	5–8	170	30–35
Rolled	3–5	170	35–40
Cushion style	3–5	170	30–35
Boston shoulder (butt)	4–6	170	40–45
Tenderloin	½–1		45–60
Back ribs		(well done)	(1½–2½ hrs.)
Spareribs		(well done)	(1½–2½ hrs.)
Pork Loaf, ground	2		(1¾ hrs.)
SMOKED			
Loin	3–5	160	25–30
Picnic shoulder (cook-before-eating)	5–8	170	35
Picnic shoulder (fully cooked)	5–8	130	25–30
Shoulder roll (butt)	2–3	170	35–40
Canadian-style bacon	2–4	160	35–40
Ham loaf (ground)	2	(total)	(½ hrs.)
Ham patties (ground)	(1 inch thick)	(total)	45–60

Serve Pork Roasts with: *tart fruit:* hot or cold apple-sauce, currant jelly, broiled peaches, broiled or glazed pineapple slices; cranberry relish; and *vegetables:* sweet potatoes, squash, yellow turnips, Irish potatoes, baked or boiled onions, sauerkraut, any kind of cabbage, and tomatoes.

Braising

Heat heavy skillet or Dutch oven. For cut with own fat, no fat need be added to pan. For lean fillets and cutlets, add 1 to 2 tablespoons lard or other fat to pan. Brown meat slowly on all sides, about 10 to 15 minutes (less for chops and steaks). Pour off excess fat. Season meat. Add ½ cup (or more) liquid. (To spareribs, add 1 or 2 cups tomato or barbecue sauce at the beginning of braising.) Cover cooker tightly. Reduce heat. Braise until meat is fork-tender and well done. Cooking time depends on size and thickness of meat.

Braising Time for Fresh Pork ★
(After Browning)

	APPROXIMATE TIME (MINUTES)
Chops	
½ inch thick	30
¾ to 1½ inches thick	45–60
Shoulder steaks, ¾ inch thick	45–60
Spareribs (2 to 3 pounds)	90

Broiling (Grilling)

Preheat broiler. Trim excess fat from chops and steaks. Slash fat edge of meat every 2 inches to prevent curling. Rub broiler rack with trimmed-off or other fat. Place meat on rack. Insert rack in broiler pan which has been lined with foil. Broil 2 to 3 inches below source of heat until meat is brown on one side. Season meat if desired; turn with tongs. Broil second side until well done. Serve at once on hot platter. For outdoor grills, follow cooker's directions for distance from heat.

The broiling time for fresh pork in the chart below is given somewhat reluctantly, for the figures do not say, "Broil with care." Otherwise, the meat may be dry and tough by the time its center is well done. Turn more often.

Broiling Time for Pork

CUT	APPROXIMATE THICKNESS (INCHES)	APPROXIMATE TIME (MINUTES)
FRESH		
Rib and loin chops	¾–1	20–25
Shoulder steaks	½–¾	20–22
Patties (ground)	1	20–25
Pork kabobs	1½ × 1½ ×	
(marinated)	¾–1	22–25
SMOKED		
Loin chops	½–¾	15–20
Bacon, Canadian-style		
sliced	¼	6–8
sliced	½	8–10
Bacon, sliced		4–5
Ham patties		
(ground)	1	16–20

Pan-Broiling

Preheat heavy skillet or griddle. Trim excess fat from meat. Rub skillet with fat. Brown meat slowly until a light crust forms. Turn with tongs or slotted pancake turner to brown second side. Add no water. Do not cover. Pour off fat as it accumulates. Reduce heat. Continue broiling until meat is well done. Turn frequently so as to cook evenly. Season. Serve at once on hot platter.

Pan-Broiling Time for Pork

| | APPROXIMATE TIME (MINUTES) | |
| | Uncooked | Cooked |
CUT	(cook-before-eating)	(fully cooked)
Smoked Picnics and Butts		
Slices		
¼ inch thick	4–6	3–4
½ inch thick	8–10	4–5
¾ inch thick	12	6

For Canadian-style and plain bacon, see time as indicated for broiling on preceding page.

For link and country-style sausages, steam first for 10 minutes in a small amount of water, and drain.

Panfrying (Sautéing) for very thin slices of tenderloin fillets, loin chops, boneless butt, Canadian-style bacon; cut-up spareribs and link sausages which have been steamed for 10 minutes and drained.

In heavy skillet, heat a small amount of fat. Brown meat on both sides. Season. Reduce heat. Cook uncovered until well done. Turn occasionally.

Be guided by time for pan-broiling.

Simmering "Boiled" Pork for large cuts. ★

Scrub meat before cooking. In large kettle, place meat and cover with cold water. Add seasonings to fresh pork. Let liquid come to boil. Remove fat and scum that rises to the top. Cover and simmer (do not boil) until meat is fork-tender. If possible, cool meat for one hour in the broth. Reserve broth for cooking beans, cabbage, and greens.

Simmering Time for Pork

CUT	APPROXIMATE WEIGHT (POUNDS)	TOTAL TIME (HOURS)
FRESH		
Spareribs		2–2½
Backbones (country style)		2–2½
Hocks		2½–3
SMOKED		
Picnic shoulder	5–8	3½–4
Shoulder roll (butt)	2–4	1½–1¾
Hocks		2½–3

NOTE: If boiled pork is pressure-cooked, follow manufacturer's time directions.

Barbecued Spareribs
(An Adapted American Indian Recipe)

Total Time: about 1¾ hours   Serves: 4 or more

2 to 3 pounds spareribs (2 racks)
Barbecue Sauce recipe
Watercress to garnish

Ask meatman to chop through ribs at large ends.

Place spareribs in shallow open pan; cover with foil. Roast in slow (325° F.) oven for 30 minutes. Pour off fat. Roast 30 minutes longer.

Meanwhile, prepare Barbecue Sauce.

Increase oven heat to hot (400° F.); uncover spareribs and roast until fork-tender, nicely browned and glazed, about 30 to 40 minutes. Baste often with sauce.

To serve: Cut spareribs, with scissors or sharp knife, into serving pieces. Garnish with watercress. Serve at once with parslied potatoes and sauerkraut.

Barbecue Sauce (Cooked) ★

Total Time: about 30 minutes   Yield: about 2 cups

    2 tablespoons butter or margarine
    ½ cup chopped onions
    1 can (6 ounces) tomato paste
    1 can (6 ounces) water or red wine
    ½ cup cider vinegar
    ¼ cup unsulphured molasses
    1 teaspoon salt
    1 teaspoon Worcestershire sauce
    ½ teaspoon Tabasco

Melt fat in saucepan; add onions and sauté until limp,
about 10 minutes. Add remaining ingredients; bring to a
rolling boil. Simmer for 10 minutes; *stir often.*

Pot-Roasted Spareribs ★

Total Time: about 2½ hours   Serves: 4 or more

    2 to 3 pounds spareribs (2 racks)
    ¼ cup flour
    1 tablespoon salt
    ½ teaspoon paprika
    ⅛ teaspoon black pepper
    2 tablespoons fat
    2 carrots, scraped and halved
    1 celery stalk and leaves
    1 large tomato, halved
    1 medium onion, pricked with fork
    ¾ cup sherry or red wine
    2 tablespoons water
    Dash Tabasco

Cut spareribs in halves; dredge thoroughly with combined flour, salt, paprika and pepper.

In Dutch oven or large heavy skillet, heat fat. Brown meat on all sides, about 15 minutes. Remove excess fat. Place rack under meat in cooker. Put vegetables on meat. Blend wine with water and add to meat.

Cover tightly. Braise over low heat until meat is tender, about 1½ to 2 hours.

Place spareribs on hot platter; keep hot. Press vegetables through a sieve. Remove excess fat from meat juices; see shortcut on page 252. Add puréed vegetables and Tabasco to meat juices; reheat. Cut spareribs in serving pieces and cover with sauce.

Serve with buttered green peas and mashed potatoes sprinkled with paprika.

Cantonese Pork Stew ★

Total Time: 1½ hours   Serves: 4 to 6

  1½ pounds boned fresh pork shoulder
    2 tablespoons fat or oil
    1 can (9 ounces) pineapple chunks, undrained
  ⅓ cup wine vinegar
  ½ cup chopped onions
  ¼ cup chopped green pepper
    2 tablespoons cornstarch
  ¼ cup cold water
    1 tablespoon soy sauce
  ¼ cup brown sugar
    2 tablespoons apricot jam (optional)
    3 to 4 cups hot steamed rice
    1 tablespoon minced parsley

Trim excess fat from meat; slice into thin strips.

In Dutch oven or heavy skillet, heat fat. Sauté pork until golden brown on all sides, about 15 minutes. Turn often. Drain excess fat.

Mix pineapple liquid with enough water to make 1½ cups. Blend in vinegar, onion, pepper and pineapple chunks. Pour mixture over meat. Cover tightly and braise over low heat until meat is tender, about 1 hour.

Meanwhile blend cornstarch with water and soy sauce. Stir into meat mixture. Cook, stirring constantly, until sauce is clear and slightly thickened, about 2 minutes. Blend in sugar and jam; simmer until dissolved.

Place meat on heated platter. Toss cooked rice with fork and arrange in ring around meat. Sprinkle with parsley.

Serve immediately with tossed green salad. *NOTE:* If you cook ahead, thicken sauce after reheating.

Umani ★
(A Pork Stew from Tahiti)

Total Time: about 1 hour   Serves: 4 to 6

    1½ pounds lean pork, cut in ½-inch cubes
     2 cups bouillon or water
     1 large carrot, scraped and diced
     1 can (8½ ounces) bamboo shoots, sliced or cubed
     2 cans (5 ounces each) water chestnuts, sliced
     1 can (16 ounces) cut green beans
     1 can (6 ounces) sliced or whole mushrooms
    ¼ cup soy sauce
     3 to 4 cups hot steamed brown rice

In large skillet, bring pork and bouillon to boil; skim off fat and scum. Cover and simmer until meat is almost tender, about 30 minutes.

Add carrot, bamboo shoots and water chestnuts; cover and simmer for 10 minutes. Add green beans, mushrooms and soy sauce. Cover and simmer for 10 minutes.

Serve piping hot with brown rice in separate dish.

Pork Steaks with Spicy Prunes ★

Total Time: about 1¼ hours   Serves: 4

    20 pitted prunes
    20 whole cloves
     4 pork shoulder steaks, ¾ inch thick
    Salt and pepper to taste
     1 tablespoon fat
    ½ cup chopped onions
    ½ cup Burgundy or red wine
    1½ tablespoons lemon juice
     1 teaspoon cornstarch
     1 tablespoon cold water

Rinse prunes and stick each with a clove. Sprinkle steaks with salt and pepper. In heavy skillet, heat fat and brown meat on both sides, turning frequently, for 10 minutes. Add onion; cover and sauté over low heat for 5 minutes. Add wine and lemon juice; blend well. Add prunes and stir lightly.

Cover tightly. Braise over low heat until meat is tender, 45 to 60 minutes. Remove steaks and prunes to preheated platter; keep hot.

Blend cornstarch with water; stir into meat juices. Cook and stir until thickened. Pour over steaks and serve at once with mixed vegetables and steamed rice.

Breaded Pork Chops or Steaks

Total Time: about 1½ hours   Serves: 6

  ¾ cup milk
  1 egg, slightly beaten
  ½ teaspoon salt
  6 pork chops or shoulder steaks, ¾ inch thick
    About 3 cups dry bread crumbs
  4 tablespoons fat or oil
  ¼ teaspoon dried savory or thyme
  1 cup bouillon or ½ cup white wine and
  ½ cup water
  ¼ cup chopped onions
    Milk (optional)
  3 tablespoons flour (optional)

In flat dish, blend milk with egg and salt. Dip meat in milk mixture, then in bread crumbs; coat well. In heavy skillet, heat fat; sauté meat quickly, turning once. Add savory, bouillon and onions. Cover tightly. Reduce heat and braise until meat is tender, about 45 to 60 minutes; turn once. Remove meat to heated platter; keep hot.

If a thickened gravy is desired, add milk to pan drippings to make 2 cups. Mix 3 tablespoons flour with 3 tablespoons water to a smooth paste; add and cook, stirring constantly, until gravy has thickened. Season to taste.

Pour gravy over meat or serve in separate dish with parslied potatoes and buttered peas.

Hungarian Zuitzi
(Pork Chop Casserole)

Total Time: about 2 hours   Serves: 6

        4 tablespoons butter or margarine
        1 cup chopped onions
        2 large potatoes, peeled and thinly sliced
    1½ teaspoons salt
    1½ teaspoons Hungarian paprika
        3 large tomatoes, peeled and sliced
        2 cups regular rice, washed and drained
        3 green peppers, seeded and sliced
        6 pork chops (shoulder or loin), 1 inch thick
        2 cups water or bouillon
        2 cups red wine
        Parsley sprigs

In casserole, heat butter; add onions and potatoes; sauté until onions are golden brown, stirring frequently, about 10 minutes. Sprinkle with a little salt and paprika.

Cover with tomatoes. Spread rice on top. Cover with green pepper slices. Sprinkle each layer with a little salt and paprika.

Meanwhile, sauté pork chops in their own fat, about 10 minutes; turn often to brown evenly. If necessary, add 1 tablespoon fat to skillet.

Place meat on top of food in casserole. Add enough water and wine to reach the green peppers. Do not cover meat with liquid.

Bake, covered, in a moderate (375° F.) oven until meat is tender, about 1 to 1¼ hours. Add more liquid after 45 minutes baking, if necessary. Garnish with parsley.

Serve with cole slaw or Boston lettuce.

Pork and Apple Casserole ★

Total Time: about 2 hours   Serves: 6

- 6 shoulder pork chops
- 1 cup chopped onions
- 6 medium tart apples, cored and sliced 1 inch thick
- ¼ cup brown sugar
- 1 teaspoon salt (more or less to taste)
- ¼ teaspoon black pepper (more or less to taste)
- ½ cup bouillon or consommé (or more)
- 1 tablespoon butter or margarine (optional)
- ⅛ teaspoon nutmeg

Trim excess fat from meat. Cover bottom of a slightly greased wide (2-quart) casserole with one-half the onions; top with one-half the apples; sprinkle with one-half the sugar. Put chops on top; season with salt and pepper. Cover remaining onions, then with a mixture of apples and sugar. Season again with salt and pepper.

Pour bouillon over food. Dot with butter and sprinkle with nutmeg.

Cover casserole. Bake in a moderate (350° F.) oven until meat is well done, about 1½ to 1¾ hours, depending on thickness of chops.

Serve with baked or mashed potatoes and steamed parslied carrots. *NOTE:* If you cook ahead, bake for 1½ hours and reheat with ½ cup bouillon.

Smoked Pork with Raisin Sauce ★

Total Time:
See *Simmering Time for Pork,* page 132, or follow wrapper directions

One Serving:
bone-in meat, ½ to ¾ pound; boned meat, ⅓ to ½ pound; hocks, ¾ to 1 pound

Pork hock, picnic shoulder or boneless shoulder butt
Raisin Sauce recipe

Wash meat thoroughly before cooking or follow wrapper directions. Place meat in Dutch oven or deep large kettle; cover with cold water. Bring to boil. Skim off fat and scum. Cover and simmer (do not boil) until meat is tender.

If possible, cool meat in broth for 1 hour. Save cooking liquid for cooking beans and cabbage. Slice to serve with jacket-potatoes and cabbage. Serve with Raisin Sauce in separate dish.

Raisin Sauce ★

Total Time: about 15 minutes   Yield: about 2 cups

Mix ½ cup sugar with 2 tablespoons cornstarch and ¼ teaspoon salt; add to 2 cups apple juice and ½ cup seedless raisins in a saucepan. Tie four small pieces of cinnamon stick and eight whole cloves in a large piece of cheesecloth; add. Cover and simmer for about 10 minutes. Remove spice bag. Serve hot.

Pigs' Knuckles and Kraut ★

Total Time: 3 to 4 hours   Serves: 6 or more

  6 pigs' knuckles
  2 quarts sauerkraut, canned or in bulk
  2 teaspoons caraway seeds
  1 teaspoon celery seeds
  Beer, ale or water

Wash and scrape pigs' knuckles; drain.
In Dutch oven or large heavy kettle, place one-half

sauerkraut; add meat and sprinkle with caraway seeds. Blend celery seeds with remaining sauerkraut and spoon over meat. Cover with beer. Cover and simmer over low heat until knuckles are tender, about 3 to 4 hours. Serve with boiled potatoes.

NOTE: This dish may be prepared with shredded red cabbage instead of sauerkraut; or with 1 quart each of sauerkraut and red cabbage.

THE STORY OF HAM

Fresh ham—known as "fresh ham" on the East coast of America and in Canada, as "leg of pork" on the West coast, and as "pork leg" in the South—is cooked much the same way as pork loin. It is a favorite with many, even though it is less popular than smoked ham.

Smoked ham is an all-year favorite in three different styles: *Cook-before-eating* ham, which must be thoroughly cooked; *ready-to-eat* ham, which is safe to eat as it is, though further light cooking improves its flavor and texture; and *fully cooked* ham, which may be heated before serving. *Canned* hams are fully cooked.

Hams usually carry an identifying label with complete cooking instructions. If the label is not present, ask the meatman.

The following chart gives you a bird's-eye view of the wide variety in ham styles.

The Styles of Smoked Ham

Ham	Kinds Available	Description
Regular shank-on	cook-before-eating ready to eat fully cooked	contains leg and shank bones; with skin on
Skinless and shankless	cook-before-eating ready to eat fully cooked	bony shank removed; skinless; with some fat trimmed
Boneless roll	cook-before-eating fully cooked	boneless; skinless; very little fat
Canned	fully cooked	boneless and skinless; may be refrigerated (unopened) up to 1 year

How to Estimate Cost for a Ham Serving

In terms of actual servings, there is not too much difference in the cost of the different styles of ham. On an equal-quality-and-weight basis, here are some guidelines to figure cost. Uncooked hams are usually less expensive than fully cooked hams. Hams with skin-on and bone-in are usually less expensive than skinned and (partially or fully) boned hams. Shank halves with center cuts sliced off usually cost less than butt halves. Center slices, the choice part of the ham, cost more per pound than a whole or half ham.

How to Plan Ham Servings

A rule of thumb: You need twice the weight of bone-in ham that you need of boneless ham.

Cut	One Average Serving
Fresh	about ½ lb.
Smoked	
bone-in	½–¾ lb.
boneless	about ¼ lb.

How to Store Ham

For step-by-step directions to store ham, see *Meat Storage in Transit*. See also *Carving Made Easy*.

How to Bake Ham
(Basic Recipe)

Plan to rest the baked ham for about 15 minutes before carving and serving.

1. Preheat oven to 325° F. Place ham, fat side up, on rack in a shallow open roasting pan. Insert meat thermometer in center of thickest part of meat; check that the bulb does not touch bone or fat.

2. Bake until ham is well done and meat thermometer registers the desired internal temperature:

cook-before-eating hams	160° F.
ready-to-eat hams	140° F.
fully cooked hams	130° F.

For a more succulent ham, baste with ½ cup club soda or ginger ale once or twice during baking. For approximate time, see chart below.

3. One-half hour before ham is well done, prepare to glaze. Remove ham from oven. Remove meat thermometer. Pour off meat juices. Peel off shank skin if present. Score ham in diamond shapes and stud with whole cloves, if desired.

4. Spread glaze on ham. Reinsert thermometer. Return ham to oven. Continue baking in a very hot (450° F.)

oven until brown; recheck internal temperature. Meanwhile, remove excess fat from meat juices and reheat.

To serve: Place ham on preheated platter and meat juices in separate dish. Serve with buttered green beans or peas and whipped mashed potatoes.

Guide to
Baking Time For Smoked Ham
(in 325° F. oven)

	TIME	
	(IN HOURS)	
	Internal Temperature	
WEIGHT	160° F.	130° F.
(IN POUNDS)	cook-before-eating	fully cooked*
Whole (bone-in)		
8–10	3¼–3½	2–2¼
10–12	3½–3¾	2¼–2½
12–15	3¾–4½	2½–3
15–18	4¼–4¾	3–3½
18–22	5–6	3½–4¼
24	6½	4¼–4½
Whole (boneless)		
10–12	3¾–4	1½–1¾
12–14	4–4½	2
Half (bone-in)		
5–8	3–3½+	1½–2
Half (boneless)		
5–8	2½–3½	1½–2
Slices		
2 inch	1	⅔

Canned ham (removed from can) requires 15 to 20 minutes per pound.

*For ready-to-eat ham, time may be a bit longer; internal temperature must be 140° F.

+Shank half needs a little less cooking time than butt half.

How to Glaze Baked Ham
(Basic Recipe)

After ham has been skinned and scored, spread evenly with any of the following glazes. Make certain that there are no "empty" spots.

Pineapple Glaze ★: Mix 1 cup light brown sugar thoroughly with 1 teaspoon dry mustard which has been moistened with 1 tablespoon pineapple juice; add about ¼ cup each of crushed pineapple and applesauce; blend with 1 teaspoon vinegar or orange juice.

Orange Glaze ★: Mix 1 cup honey with ½ cup orange marmalade and moisten with orange juice to spreading consistency.

Mustard Glaze ★: Mix 1 cup jelly with ½ teaspoon prepared mustard and moisten with red wine.

Spiced currant Glaze ★: Mix 1 cup currant jelly or jellied cranberry sauce with 1 teaspoon dry mustard, ¼ teaspoon (ground) cloves, ¼ teaspoon cinnamon and 2 tablespoons vinegar or wine.

How to Broil Smoked Ham Slices
(Basic Recipe)

Set oven regulator for broiling. Slash fat edges of ham. Place on greased broiler rack in broiler pan lined with foil. Broil at proper distance from source of heat until well done and lightly browned. For approximate broiling time, see chart below. Turn once or twice with tongs or slotted pancake turner. Brush after last turning with a glaze, if desired; see *Index* for glaze recipes. Serve at once.

Guide to
Broiling Time for Ham Slices

KIND	DISTANCE FROM HEAT (IN INCHES)	APPROXIMATE TIME ON EACH SIDE (IN MINUTES)
Fully cooked		
½ inch thick	2	3
1 inch thick		
(center slice)	3–5	5–6
1½ inches thick	5–6	10–12
Cook-before-eating		
½ inch thick	2–3	8–10
1 inch thick	3–5	10–15

For cook-before-eating ham slices that are 1½ inches thick, do not broil; instead, bake in a slow (325° F.) oven for about 1½ hours.

How to Pan-Broil Smoked Ham Slices
(Basic Recipe)

Preheat heavy skillet or griddle. Trim excess fat from ham. Rub skillet with fat. Cook slices slowly until light brown. Turn frequently with tongs or slotted pancake turner. Add no water. Do not cover. Pour off fat as it accumulates. Reduce heat if necessary. Broil until well done. Serve at once on heated platter.

Guide to
Pan-Broiling Time for Ham Slices

THICKNESS	MINUTES ON EACH SIDE	
	Fully cooked	Cook-before-eating
¼ inch	2	4–6
½ inch	4–5	8–10
¾ inch	6	12

How to Simmer Smoked Boiled Ham ★
(Basic Recipe)

Remove any casings. In large kettle, place ham and cover with cold water. Let liquid come to boil. Remove fat and scum that rise to top. If ham is very salty, discard water and start once again.

Cover and simmer until ham is tender. For approximate simmering time, see chart below.

Guide to
Simmering Time for Smoked Ham

CUT	AVERAGE WEIGHT (IN POUNDS)	APPROXIMATE COOKING TIME (IN MINUTES PER POUND)
Old-style & country cured		
Large	12–16	20
Small	10–12	25
Half	5–8	30
Tendered (smoked)		
Shank or butt half	5–8	20–25

Glazed Ham with Frozen Horseradish
and Cumberland Sauce
(A Traditional Austrian Dinner)

Baked ham

Choice of Glazes:
    Apricot Glaze or Currant-Mustard Glaze recipe
Frozen Horseradish recipe
Cumberland Sauce recipe

Bake any kind ham of your choice. Follow step-by-step directions, *How to Bake Ham,* page 143.
Glaze with either one of the two glazes.
Serve with buttered egg noodles, frozen horseradish and Cumberland sauce. If ham is smaller, use one-half glaze recipe.

Apricot Glaze ★: Blend ½ cup white corn syrup with 1½ cups apricot jam. Season to taste with a dash of Tabasco. Yield: about 2 cups glaze.

Currant-Mustard Glaze ★: Blend ½ cup prepared mustard into 2 cups currant jelly. Yield: about 2 cups glaze.

Frozen Horseradish ★

Total Time: about 30 minutes;   Serves: 8 or more
to chill, overnight   Yield: 1 quart

    2 envelopes unflavored gelatin
    1 cup cold water
    ¼ cup sugar
    2 teaspoons salt
    1½ cups (3 4-ounce bottles) prepared horseradish
    1½ cups heavy cream, whipped

In saucepan or top part of double boiler, soften gelatin in cold water. Add combined sugar, salt and horseradish; blend well. Place over boiling water and stir until gelatin and sugar are dissolved. Chill over iced water until mixture is slightly thicker than the consistency of unbeaten egg whites. Fold mixture into whipped cream.

Turn into an oiled 1-quart mold and chill until firm, about 2 hours, or better, overnight. Unmold to serve with ham.

Cumberland Sauce ★

Total Time: about 10   Yield: about 2 cups sauce
minutes; 3 hours to chill

In a deep bowl, blend the contents of one can (1 pound) jellied cranberry sauce with one glass (12 ounces) currant jelly, the juice and rind of one lemon and one orange, 1 tablespoon dry mustard and salt to taste. Chill for at least 3 hours before serving. Place in attractive glass dish to serve with ham.

Baked Ham with Orange Glaze

Total Time: 15–20 minutes   Serves: about ¼ pound
per pound; and 30 minutes   for one serving
for preparation

Canned ham
Orange Glaze; see *Index*
Whole cloves (optional)

Preheat oven to 325° F. Place ham on rack in shallow roasting pan and bake in a slow oven, allowing 12 to 15 minutes for each pound. One-half hour before heating is completed, remove ham from oven. Score diamond shapes or score with a small cooky cutter. Spread orange glaze on ham. If ham is large, double the glaze recipe. Stud with cloves, if desired. Return to oven for one-half hour.

Serve with sweet potatoes and buttered green peas.

Pineapple-Glazed Ham Roll

Total Time: about 2 hours   Serves: about ¼ pound
                                                for one serving

    3 to 4-pound fully cooked boneless ham
    Pineapple Glaze; see *Index*

Preheat oven to 325° F. Place ham on rack in a shallow roasting pan. Insert meat thermometer. Bake for 1½ to 1¾ hours, to internal meat temperature of 130° F. One-half hour before heating is completed, remove ham from oven and score. Drizzle glaze on ham. Return to oven.
    Serve with buttered baby onions and mixed vegetables.

Baked Frosted Ham Steak

Total Time: about 45 minutes   Serves: 4 to 6

    1   cup canned pineapple juice
    ½   teaspoon whole cloves
    ¼   teaspoon dry mustard
    ½   cup sour cream, stiffly whipped
        1-inch-thick ready-to-eat ham slice, about 1½ pounds

In small saucepan, blend pineapple juice with cloves and mustard. Bring to boil. Cook until liquid is reduced to one-half cup. Cool quickly; strain liquid; fold in whipped sour cream.
    Meanwhile, preheat oven to 350° F. Place ham on rack in shallow pan. Bake for 10 minutes. Turn with pancake turner.
    Spread sour cream mixture on ham. Bake until cream is lightly browned and ham well heated through, about 15 minutes.
    Serve at once on preheated platter with broiled tomatoes or steamed broccoli; and cranberry relish.

Broiled Ham Slice with Mustard Glaze

Total Time: about 25 minutes   Serves: about 6

1-inch-thick fully cooked ham slice, center cut
Mustard Glaze; see *Index*

Set oven regulator for broiling. Lightly score cut surfaces and slash fat edges of ham slice. Spread glaze on one side of ham. Place on greased broiler rack in broiler pan lined with foil. Broil 3 to 5 inches below source of heat for 5 to 6 minutes. Turn with tongs or slotted pancake turner. Top with remaining glaze and broil 5 to 6 minutes.

Serve with stewed tomatoes or mashed potatoes; and hot applesauce.

VEAL

Good-quality veal has a velvety texture and light grayish pink color. Its lean is soft and moist with very little outside fat and practically no marbling, and it is less firm than the meat of older beef. Bones are soft, porous and red.

Veal is an international favorite and cherished for its delicate taste, its true economy and its versatility. Many Americans eat veal only occasionally, partly because they do not know how to prepare it tastefully. Veal needs more seasoning than any other meat.

There are three simple steps to tasty veal dishes:

1. *Cook slowly and at low temperatures*. Moist heat or basting will break down the meat's abundant connective

tissue. To be taste-tempting, veal is best roasted or braised, not broiled.

2. *Add fat* in cooking because the meat is lean. Use salt pork or bacon on roasts; add butter, margarine or oil to pot roasts and stews.

3. *Season well* with basil, capers, fines herbes, garlic, lemon juice, marjoram, parsley, rosemary, or thyme; also dry white wine, sherry, or vermouth.

How to Plan Veal Servings

ONE AVERAGE SERVING	POUNDS FOR ONE SERVING
Bone-in meat	⅓–½
Boned meat	¼–⅓

How to Store Veal

For step-by-step directions, see *Meat Storage in Transit.*

How to Select Veal

For Roasts and Pot Roasts:

Bone-in shoulder: available with arm and blade bone, similar to beef. Have meatman cut a pocket for stuffing.

Arm roast   Blade roast
Bone-in shoulder

Boned Shoulder: rolled and tied; more economical and easier to carve than bone-in shoulder; also available frozen with brand name and cooking directions.

Rolled shoulder

Breast

Breast: a flat cut available boned and bone-in; may be stuffed.

Stuffed breast

For Chops, Steaks, and Cutlets:

Blade Chops or Steaks: with considerable bone and less-tender meat.

Blade steak or chop

Arm steak

Arm and Leg Steaks: arm steak with round bone, smaller than leg steak.

Leg steak

Cutlets: boneless, usually cut in ¼ to ½-inch thicknesses; also "Frenched," that is, flattened by pounding.

Cutlets (boneless)

"City Chicken": cubed veal steak or other boneless veal threaded on wooden or metal skewers; sometimes on special sale.

"City chicken"

Veal birds: boned steaks rolled and fastened with a skewer; sometimes on special sale. They may be re-rolled around a bread dressing, then tied and braised.

Veal birds

For stews: neck, flank, heel of round, plate, shoulder, shank; also rump when on sale.

Shanks: for braising (Osso Buco) and jelling.

Fore shank

Ground meat: to be braised, pan-fried, or baked; breast, neck, shoulder, shank, and flank meat for loaves and patties.

"Mock Chicken Legs": ground veal molded in the shape of drumsticks around a wooden skewer; to be braised.

The less-expensive cuts of veal are breast, shoulder, shank, and neck.

Roast Veal
(Basic Recipe)

Roast a boned and rolled shoulder of at least 3 pounds. If frozen, follow cooking directions on wrapper.

Plan to rest the roast for about 15 minutes before slicing and serving.

Total Time: 2–3 hours   Serves: 6 or more

1. Preheat oven to 325° F. Rub meat with cut clove garlic or a mixture of salt and rosemary. If meat has little fat covering, place several thin strips of bacon or salt pork on roast. Place, fat side up, on rack in shallow open roasting pan. Insert meat thermometer in center of roast.

2. Roast until well done, for 40 to 45 minutes per pound or to an internal temperature of 170° F. Do not cover, do not baste, do not turn meat.

3. When fork-tender, remove roast to preheated platter; sprinkle immediately with the juice of one-half lemon. Make gravy from meat juices, if desired; check the seasoning of meat juices or gravy before serving.

Serve with cranberry sauce, pickled peaches, steamed rice and a tossed green salad.

NOTE: Use same recipe for bone-in roast, allowing 35 to 40 minutes roasting time per pound.

Veal Pot Roast ★
(Basic Recipe)

Braise a boned and rolled shoulder of at least 3 pounds. If frozen, follow cooking directions on wrapper.

Plan to rest pot roast for about 15 minutes before slicing and serving.

Total Time: 2–3 hours   Serves: 6 or more

1. Season meat with salt and pepper or any other desired seasoning. Roll in flour; coat well.

2. In Dutch oven or heavy skillet, heat 3 to 4 tablespoons fat or oil. Brown meat thoroughly for 15 to 20 minutes, adding a tablespoon or two of fat, if necessary. Place rack under meat.

3. Add about 1 cup liquid (bouillon, tomato juice or wine, plain or mixed). Sprinkle with ½ teaspoon salt for each pound of meat. If desired, add a cut clove garlic, ¼ teaspoon paprika, ⅛ teaspoon white or black pepper and 1 bay leaf or ⅛ teaspoon celery seeds. Cover tightly. Braise over low heat until fork-tender, 40 to 45 minutes per pound.

4. If desired, add peeled and sliced potatoes, carrots or tomatoes about 45 minutes before meat is done.

To serve: Remove meat and vegetables (if any) to preheated platter; keep hot. For a thickened gravy, measure meat juices; add flour or cornstarch accordingly; serve in separate dish. Serve with steamed rice and creamed spinach.

If cooked ahead, follow step-by-step directions in *The Basic Beef Pot Roast*. Cook until firm-tender. Slice before reheating; add vegetables (step 4) when reheating.

NOTE: Use the same recipe for boned and stuffed veal breast.

Braising Time for Veal
(After Browning)

CUT	WEIGHT OR THICKNESS	TIME (APPROXIMATE)
Breast		
stuffed	3–4 lbs.	1½–2½ hrs.
rolled	2–3 lbs.	1½–2½ hrs.
Shoulder, rolled	3–4 lbs.	2½–3 hrs.
Veal birds	(½ ×2 ×4 in.)	45–60 min.
Chops	½–¾ in.	45–60 min.
Steaks & cutlets	½–¾ in.	45–60 min.
Shoulder chops	½–¾ in.	45–60 min.

Continental Veal Pot Roast ★

Total Time: 2½ to 3 hours   Serves: 8 or more

    1 4-pound rolled veal shoulder
    2 teaspoons salt
    ¼ teaspoon white pepper
    ¼ teaspoon dried rosemary
    ¼ teaspoon dried thyme
    ¼ cup chopped onions
    3 tablespoons oil
    Flour
    Chicken bouillon or white wine
    4 large potatoes, peeled and quartered
    1 pound (or more) whole snap beans (fresh)
    Sour cream (optional)
    Chopped parsley or mint

Cut cords on roast and unroll meat; sprinkle with salt, pepper, rosemary, thyme, onion and 1 tablespoon oil. Reroll; tie securely. Dredge veal with about ⅓ cup flour. In Dutch oven or heavy skillet, heat remaining 2 tablespoons oil. Brown meat on all sides. Place low rack under roast.

Add liquid to depth of ¾ inch. Cover tightly. Braise over low heat until tender, about 2½ to 3 hours. Turn roast once or twice during cooking.

About 30 minutes before veal is done, add potatoes and beans. Cover, and braise until vegetables and meat are tender. To make gravy, measure 1 tablespoon flour for each cup of meat juices. Blend flour with a little cold water; add to the boiling meat juices and cook, stirring constantly, until thickened. Blend in sour cream to taste.

To serve: Place veal on preheated platter; sprinkle with parsley and surround with vegetables. Serve gravy in separate dish. *NOTE:* If you cook ahead, add sour cream after reheating.

Barbecued Veal Riblets ★

Total Time: about 1¾ hours   Serves: 4 to 6

    ¼ cup bacon drippings or lard
    3 pounds veal riblets, cut in serving pieces
    Barbecue Sauce recipe

In large heavy skillet, heat lard. Brown riblets on all sides, about 10 minutes; turn often. Add barbecue sauce. Cover tightly. Braise until meat is tender, about 1½ hours.

Serve piping hot with buttered noodles and mixed vegetables.

Barbecue Sauce (Cooked) ★

Total Time: about 1 hour;   Yield: about 4 cups
prepare 24 hours before use

¾ cup butter or margarine, melted
1 cup chili sauce
¾ cup chopped onions
½ cup water
½ cup cider vinegar
1 can (8 ounces) tomato sauce
1 cup oil
2 tablespoons Worcestershire sauce
1 clove garlic, minced or puréed
¼ teaspoon dried tarragon
⅛ teaspoon black pepper

In saucepan, combine ingredients in order indicated;
bring to boil, stirring constantly. Cover and simmer over
very low heat for 1 hour. Cool. Cover and refrigerate to
"ripen." Heat before use. *NOTE:* Prepare only one-half
of recipe for less "stewlike" riblets.

Veal Madelaine ★

Total Time: about 1½ hours   Serves: 4 to 6

  2 pounds boned veal (breast or shank), cut in 1½-inch cubes
  2 tablespoons butter or margarine
  3 tablespoons flour
  1 teaspoon salt
  ¼ teaspoon white or black pepper
  2 strips lemon peel, 1 inch wide
  1 tablespoon drained (bottled) capers
  1 cup hot chicken bouillon
  ½ cup white wine
 12 small white onions, peeled
 12 new potatoes of uniform size, scraped
  1 cup light or heavy cream
  Minced fresh dill

Trim excess fat from meat. In heavy skillet, heat butter. Brown veal for 5 minutes, turning occasionally. Sprinkle meat in skillet with a mixture of flour, salt and pepper. Continue browning, turning frequently, about 10 minutes.

Add lemon peel, capers, bouillon and wine; blend. Cover tightly and braise over low heat for 30 minutes. Remove lemon peel.

Add onions and potatoes. Cover and simmer until meat and vegetables are tender, about 30 minutes. Remove vegetables to preheated platter; reserve.

Reduce heat slightly. Slowly stir in cream; heat thoroughly but do not boil.

Place veal in center of preheated platter; surround with vegetables. Sprinkle dill on meat. Serve sauce in separate dish.

Osso Buco ★

(Braised Italian Veal Shanks)

Total Time: 2 to 2½ hours   Serves: 4

  ½ cup olive or cooking oil
  1 clove garlic, puréed or finely chopped
  4 veal shanks
  3 tablespoons flour
  1 medium onion, finely chopped
  2 small carrots, finely chopped
  1 celery stalk and leaves, finely chopped
  1 can (28 ounces) whole tomatoes
  2 bay leaves
  1 cup white wine or chicken bouillon
  2 tablespoons minced parsley
  1 tablespoon finely grated lemon rind
Salt and white pepper to taste

In Dutch oven or heavy skillet, heat oil and garlic. Dust veal shanks with flour. Sauté in oil on all sides, about 15 minutes. Stand upright in cooker so that the marrow cannot fall out.

Add onion, carrots, celery, tomatoes, bay leaves and wine; blend well.

Cover tightly. Braise over low heat until tender, about 1½ to 2 hours, depending on size of shanks. Add parsley and lemon rind. Season to taste with salt and pepper.

Serve on heated platter with plain risotto or saffron rice. *NOTE:* To serve at the table, remove marrow from bones.

Borju Gulyas ★
(Hungarian Veal Goulash)

Total Time: about 2 hours   Serves: 6 or more

- 1 cup butter or margarine
- 4 to 6 large onions (about 1½ pounds), finely chopped
- 1 tablespoon Hungarian paprika
- 4 pounds veal breast, cut in 2-inch pieces
- 1 tablespoon salt
- ½ teaspoon dried marjoram
- 1 cup chicken bouillon
- 1 cup water
- 1 large piece cheesecloth
- 2 large tomatoes, quartered
- 1 green pepper, cut up
  (including seeds, core and stem)
- 4 large potatoes, peeled and diced
- 1 tablespoon lard
- 1 tablespoon Hungarian paprika
- ½ cup sour cream
- 1 teaspoon drained (bottled) capers
- 1 large dill pickle (optional)

In Dutch oven or heavy skillet, heat butter; add onions and sauté over low heat until golden brown, stirring frequently, about 10 minutes. Stir in paprika and cook 2 minutes.

Add meat, salt and marjoram; sauté for 10 minutes, stirring frequently. Add bouillon and water.

In a dampened large square cheesecloth put tomatoes and pepper; tie into a bag with long string; add to meat mixture with end of string outside of cooker. Bring liquid to boil.

Cover tightly. Reduce heat immediately and braise over low heat for 1 hour and 10 minutes.

Add potatoes and continue braising for 20 minutes. Remove cheesecloth bag.

Blend heated lard with 1 tablespoon paprika; stir in sour cream and capers. Blend slowly and lightly into gulyas. Reheat if necessary. Cut pickle into fine shreds and stir into gulyas before serving.

Serve with boiled potatoes or broad egg noodles. *NOTE:* If you cook ahead, add sour cream when reheating.

Borjutokany ★
(Transylvanian Veal Stew)

Total Time: about 1¾ hours   Serves: 4 or more

    ¼ cup lard or bacon drippings
    2 pounds veal shoulder, cut in 2-inch pieces
    1 teaspoon salt
    ½ teaspoon black pepper
    1 cup soup stock or white wine; more if needed
    1 tablespoon Hungarian paprika
    1 pound onions, finely chopped
    ½ cup soup stock or wine (optional)

In heavy skillet, heat lard; add meat, salt and pepper; blend and brown lightly, stirring constantly, about 10 minutes.

Add soup stock and paprika. Blend. Cover tightly. Braise over low heat for 1 hour.

Stir onions into meat, adding a little soup stock if needed. Cover tightly and braise until meat is tender and onions begin to brown, about 30 minutes. Should onions brown before meat is tender, add ½ cup soup stock and blend.

Serve piping hot with buttered broad noodles and cucumber salad.

Belgian Veal and Endive Casserole

Total Time: about 1¾ hours   Serves: 6 or more

    4 pounds veal breast, cut in 2-inch pieces
    ½ tablespoon salt
    ¼ teaspoon black pepper
    ¼ cup butter or margarine
    ½ cup flour (approximate)
    3 endives

Trim excess fat from meat. Mix salt and pepper and
sprinkle on meat. In casserole, melt butter; brown meat on
all sides, about 10 minutes. Wash, trim and cut endives in
halves; place around meat.

Butter a piece of brown paper and place over casserole.
Bake in a slow (325° F.) oven for about 1½ hours, basting occasionally with liquid formed in casserole. When
veal is brown and tender, there should be very little liquid
left.

Heap veal in center of preheated platter; arrange endive
at each end. (If endive is not readily available, use twelve
small heart stalks of celery [about 2 pounds] instead.)
Pour gravy over meat. Serve with steamed rice or mashed
potatoes.

Savory Veal Loaf ★

Total Time: about 1¾ hours   Serves: 6 to 8

    2 pounds ground veal
    ¼ pound salt pork, ground
    ½ cup fine dry bread crumbs
    ½ cup milk (or more)
    ½ green pepper, finely chopped
    2 tablespoons minced parsley
    1 teaspoon dried marjoram, savory, or thyme
    ¼ teaspoon black pepper
    4 hard-cooked eggs, peeled

Have veal and salt pork ground at least twice.

In large mixing bowl, blend meat with all ingredients except eggs; add a few more tablespoons milk, if necessary. Let mixture rest for a few minutes.

Press one-half of mixture into a greased ($9\times5\times3$-inch) loaf pan. On it place whole eggs, end to end in a row, in center of pan. Cover with the remaining meat mixture. Press loaf into shape gently yet firmly.

Bake in a moderate (350° F.) oven until done, about 1¼ to 1½ hours. Unmold before serving.

Serve hot or cold with a tossed green salad and crusty Italian bread.

Blanquette de Veau ★
(Blanket of Veal, a French Specialty)

Total Time: 2 to 2½ hours   Serves: 4 or more

    2 pounds veal shoulder or breast
    1 teaspoon salt
    4 cups boiling water
    1 cup finely chopped onions
    1 medium carrot, sliced
    2 whole cloves
    2 sprigs parsley
    1 bay leaf
   ¼ teaspoon white pepper
    1 tablespoon butter or margarine
    2 tablespoons flour
   ½ cup sliced mushrooms, fresh or canned
   ½ cup heavy cream (slightly more, if desired)
    1 egg yolk
    1 teaspoon lemon juice
   ⅛ teaspoon nutmeg
    1 tablespoon minced parsley

Cut meat into twelve pieces. Place in Dutch oven or

large skillet. Add salt and boiling water. Bring to quick boil; skim.

Add onions, carrot, cloves, parsley, bay leaf and pepper. Cover and simmer until meat is tender, about 1½ hours. Remove meat to preheated platter; keep hot. Strain broth.

In another saucepan, heat butter; stir in flour and sauté until smooth, stirring constantly. Add strained broth and mushrooms. Cover and simmer over low heat for 15 minutes, stirring occasionally.

In small bowl, blend cream and egg yolk; slowly stir in 4 to 6 tablespoons sauce from pan, 1 tablespoon at a time.

Stir cream mixture into sauce in pan. Add lemon juice, nutmeg and parsley. Heat but do not boil. Add salt and pepper to taste.

To serve: Place veal in center of heated platter; cover with sauce. Serve with steamed rice (as in France) or with buttered noodles. *NOTE:* If you cook ahead, cream-egg mixture should be added after reheating.

Wiener Schnitzels ★

(Breaded Veal Cutlets—A Viennese Specialty)

This is the only recipe in the book that uses a more expensive meat cut, except when on sale. However, schnitzels are so delicious that the author simply could not resist. All other recipe ingredients are quite economical.

Do not prepare one-half of recipe. Leftover schnitzels are excellent when served cold with a lemon wedge and hot toast.

Total Time: about 30 minutes   Serves: about 8

> 3 veal cutlets, about ½ inch thick
>   (about 2 pounds)
> Flour (about 1 cup)
> 3 eggs
> ¼ cup cold milk
> ¼ teaspoon salt
> ¼ teaspoon white pepper
> 2 cups sieved fine dry bread crumbs
> Lard or shortening for frying
> 8 lemon wedges
> Parsley sprigs
> Viennese Cucumber Salad recipe

Have meatman trim meat, remove bone and cut meat into at least eight pieces; then pound each piece until ⅛ inch thick or about 6 to 8 inches in size.

At home, place each piece between waxed paper and flatten it paper thin, using a mallet or rolling pin. Chill meat in waxed-paper wrapping.

Put flour on one platter. In a fairly deep bowl, mix eggs with milk, salt and pepper. Place bread crumbs in a third shallow dish or plate.

Dredge each piece of meat separately with flour; shake off excess. Using a fork, dip meat piece by piece into egg mixture; make certain that meat is well coated and that there are no "empty" spots. Using a fork again, coat meat pieces well and evenly with crumbs; shake off excess.

Heat enough fat in heavy wide skillet ½ to ¾ inch deep. It is important that the schnitzels almost swim in fat; otherwise they may stick.

Sauté schnitzels until well browned and slightly puffed, about 5 to 7 minutes on each side. If desired, keep cooked schnitzels in an oven set at 250° F. until all meat is cooked and ready to serve.

Serve with Viennese cucumber salad and skillet-fried sliced potatoes. *NOTE:* If you wish, schnitzels may be breaded ahead of serving time and refrigerated between waxed paper.

Viennese Cucumber Salad ★

Total Time: about 45 minutes   Serves: about 8

   3 large or 4 medium firm cucumbers
1½ tablespoons salt
   1 cup sour cream
Juice of ½ lemon
Hungarian paprika

Score cucumbers lengthwise with fork and slice very thin. Place in small bowl; sprinkle with salt; cover and let stand for ½ hour.

Drain cucumbers and (with your hands) press out all water. Add sour cream mixed with lemon juice; mix and chill. Sprinkle generously with paprika before serving.

NOTE: If this dish is prepared ahead, mix chilled drained cucumber with chilled sour cream shortly before serving.

DISHES WITH MIXED MEATS

Veal Galantine ★
(English Boiled Meat Loaf)

Total Time: 3½ hours   Serves: 4 to 6

Prepare one day ahead of serving

    1 veal breast, boned
    1 pound sausage meat
    2 slices bacon, diced
    2 hard-cooked eggs, peeled

For soup stock:
Veal bones
    2 carrots
    2 onions
    2 stalks celery
    2 peppercorns

Flatten veal and place skin side down; spread with sausage and bacon. Place eggs tip to tip on wide end. Roll tightly. Roll in buttered cheesecloth and fasten with string or toothpicks.

In large kettle, bring 2 quarts water to rolling boil. Add veal roll and soup vegetables. Cover and simmer over low heat for 3 hours.

Remove meat. Drain and tighten cheesecloth. Weigh down with heavy platter. Cool for several hours or, better, overnight.

To serve: Remove cheesecloth. Place cold loaf on a large platter and garnish with tomato slices, French fried potatoes and green pepper rings. Serve prepared horse-radish in separate dish.

Chinese Chow Mein

Total Time: about 1½ hours   Serves: 6

      ¼ cup oil
      1 pound lean pork, cut in 1-inch cubes
      ½ pound veal, cut in 1-inch cubes
      2 cups boiling water
      1 cup sliced onions
      2 cups diced celery
      1 teaspoon salt
      ½ cup sliced water chestnuts (canned)
      ½ cup sliced bamboo shoots (canned)
      1 can (1 pound) bean sprouts, rinsed
            and drained
      1 tablespoon unsulphured molasses
      1 tablespoon soy sauce
      1 tablespoon cornstarch
      ½ cup cold water (about)
      6 green onions
      2 cans (3 ounces each) chow mein noodles

In Dutch oven or heavy skillet, heat oil; add meats and brown well on all sides, about 10 minutes. Add water. Cover and simmer until meat is tender, about 1 hour.

Add onions, celery and salt; cover and bring to a quick boil; cook for 5 minutes.

Stir in water chestnuts, bamboo shoots and bean sprouts; mix well and bring to boil.

Add molasses, soy sauce and cornstarch which has been blended to a smooth paste with 6 tablespoons water; stir. Cover and simmer for 15 minutes.

Meanwhile, cut green onions into thin strips. Heat noodles in opened cans in a moderate (350° F.) oven until crisp, about 5 minutes.

Place chow mein in preheated serving dish; garnish with

green onions. Arrange noodles in a circle around rim of dish. Serve at once.

Szekely Gulyas ★
(Sauerkraut Goulash)

Total Time: about 1¾ hours   Serves: 6 to 8

    2 tablespoons lard or bacon fat
    2 pounds sauerkraut, bulk or canned
    1 teaspoon caraway seeds
    2 to 3 pounds stewing meat
         (a combination of pork, veal, and beef)
    1 cup chopped onions
    2 tablespoons Hungarian paprika
    Grated rind of ½ lemon
    1 teaspoon minced dill
    ½ cup white wine
    1 cup canned tomatoes
    4 skinless frankfurters, diced
    1 cup heavy or sour cream
    1 teaspoon Hungarian paprika

In Dutch oven or heavy skillet, heat lard; add sauerkraut and caraway seeds; blend and sauté for 5 minutes. Cover and simmer for 15 minutes.

Add meat, onion, paprika, lemon rind and dill. Blend wine with tomatoes; add to meat mixture; blend again.

Cover tightly. Braise over very low heat until meat is tender, about 1¼ hours. Add frankfurters; mix well.

Shortly before serving, blend heavy cream with paprika and stir slowly into gulyas. Serve piping hot with new potatoes or Teaspoon Dumplings; for recipe see *Index*. *NOTE:* If you cook ahead, add cream after reheating.

Steamed Hungarian Meat Loaf

Total Time: about 2 hours   Serves: 4 to 6

Tomato Sauce:

1 can (No. 2½) tomatoes
½ cup chopped onions
¼ cup chopped green peppers
¼ cup red wine
 Salt and black pepper to taste
1 teaspoon sugar

Meat Loaf:

2 slices white bread
½ cup water or bouillon
1 pound ground beef
½ pound ground pork
1 egg, slightly beaten
2 teaspoons salt
¼ teaspoon paprika

In deep skillet or saucepan, blend tomato sauce ingredients and bring to boil.

To prepare meat loaf: cover bread with water and squeeze dry. Mix well with remaining ingredients and shape into a ball. Tie loosely in several thicknesses of scalded cheesecloth.

Simmer, covered, in tomato sauce for 1½ hours. Slice to serve with sauce in separate dish. Serve with mixed vegetables and cucumber salad.

Köttbullar
(Swedish Meat Balls)

Total Time: about 30 minutes   Serves: 6

1½ pounds twice-ground meat
        (combination of beef, pork and veal)
¼ cup finely chopped onions
2 tablespoons minced parsley
½ cup fine dry bread crumbs
1½ teaspoons salt
¼ teaspoon white or black pepper
½ teaspoon Worcestershire sauce (optional)
½ cup water or bouillon
¼ cup butter or margarine
1 cup sour cream

In deep bowl, mix meat with onion, parsley, bread crumbs, salt, pepper and Worcestershire sauce; add water and blend thoroughly. Shape into walnut-sized balls with wet hands.

In heavy skillet, heat butter. Sauté meat balls until brown on all sides. Turn balls and shake skillet often.

After 15 minutes, remove meat to heated platter. Keep hot. Stir sour cream slowly into pan juices; heat but do not boil. Pour sauce over meat balls; serve at once with buttered broad noodles or jacket potatoes; and cucumber salad.

Kodboller
(Danish Meat Balls)

Total Time: about 30 minutes   Serves: 6

  1½ pounds twice-ground meat
        (combination of beef, pork and veal)
   ¼ cup finely chopped onions
   2 eggs, slightly beaten
   1 teaspoon salt
   ¼ teaspoon white pepper
   1 cup flour

In deep bowl, mix meat with onion to an almost smooth paste. Add remaining ingredients in order given; blend well after each addition. With wet hands, form mixture into twelve firm balls.

Drop each ball separately into boiling water. Simmer, uncovered, until meat is tender, about 15 minutes; keep in water until ready to serve.

Serve soon with boiled dilled potatoes and a tossed green salad.

German Meat Balls

Total Time: about 30 minutes   Serves: 4

   ½ pound ground beef
   ½ pound ground pork
   2 tablespoons finely chopped onion
   1 teaspoon salt
   ¼ teaspoon dried marjoram
   ¼ cup dry bread crumbs
   1 egg, slightly beaten
     Flour
   1 cup beer
   1 cup water
   2 tablespoons flour (optional)
   1 lemon, sliced or cut into wedges

If possible, have meat ground twice.

In bowl, blend the meats with onion, salt, marjoram, bread crumbs and egg; mix very well.

With wet hands, shape mixture into 1-inch balls; roll in flour.

In saucepan, bring beer and water to boil. Add meat balls. Cover and simmer over low heat until meat balls are tender, 15 to 20 minutes.

If a thickened gravy is desired, mix flour with ¼ cup cold water. Add to broth and simmer until thickened, stirring constantly. Pour gravy over meat balls. Serve at once. Serve with boiled potatoes and lemon slices in separate dish.

MISCELLANEOUS MEAT AND SAUSAGE DISHES

Oxtail Stew ★

Total Time: about 3 hours   Serves: 4 or more

- 3 tablespoons fat
- ¾ cup chopped onions
- 2 pounds disjointed oxtails, about
       1½ to 2 inches long
- 3 tablespoons plus 2 teaspoons flour
- 2 cups beef bouillon
- 3 cups cooked tomatoes, fresh or canned
- 1 tablespoon cider vinegar
- 2 teaspoons salt
- ¼ teaspoon black or white pepper
- 3 carrots, sliced
- 1 cup diced celery, stalks and leaves
- ½ cup chopped green pepper
- 2 teaspoons butter or margarine

In large heavy skillet, heat fat; add onions and sauté 5 minutes, stirring occasionally. Meanwhile, dredge oxtails with 3 tablespoons flour; add to onions and brown well on all sides, turning frequently with tongs, about 10 minutes. Add bouillon, tomatoes, vinegar, salt and pepper; blend well.

Cover tightly. Braise over low heat for 2 hours.

Add carrots, celery and green pepper. Cover and braise until meat and vegetables are tender, about 30 minutes.

Remove meat and vegetables to preheated platter; keep hot. Remove excess fat from liquid, if necessary; see *Index* for time-saving hint. Season liquid to taste.

Cream butter with remaining 2 teaspoons flour. Stir into liquid left in skillet. Bring to a quick boil while stirring. Boil 1 minute. Pour gravy over meat and vegetables. Serve immediately with rice, mashed potatoes, baked barley or kidney beans.

Bologna Barbecue

Total Time: about 30 minutes   Serves: 6 to 8

9-inch piece bologna sausage, about
   3 inches in diameter, casing removed
Whole cloves
Barbecue sauce recipe

1. *Cooked on outdoor grill:* Follow manufacturer's directions for grill. Do not stud sausage with cloves. Place bologna on spit; brush generously with barbecue sauce. Baste with more sauce every 10 minutes, until bologna is browned and heated through.

2. *On spit in an electric rotisserie:* Stud sausage with cloves. Place on skewer spit according to manufacturer's directions. Brush generously with barbecue sauce. Barbecue at medium heat for about 30 minutes, brushing every 10 minutes with more barbecue sauce.

3. *Broil in oven:* Stud sausage with cloves. Place bologna on long skewers. Brush generously with barbecue sauce. Broil 6 to 8 inches below source of heat for 25 to 30 minutes, turning and basting every 5 to 10 minutes. Reduce broiling heat in case bologna browns too fast.

Serve at once with green beans and home-fried potatoes or corn chips.

Barbecue Sauce (Uncooked) ★

Total Time: about 30 minutes, including "resting"

Yield: about 1½ cups sauce

Blend together ¼ cup cider vinegar, 1 cup tomato sauce, 3 tablespoons brown sugar or honey, ½ clove garlic (minced or puréed), ¼ teaspoon Worcestershire sauce and a dash of Tabasco.

Sweet-Sour Hot Dog Stew

Total Time: about 30 minutes

Serves: 6 to 8

- 18 medium skinless frankfurters, cut into thirds
- 1 cup chopped onions
- 2 cloves garlic, mashed
- 2 cups tomato sauce
- ½ cup pineapple juice
- 3 green peppers, sliced or chopped
- 1 can (14 ounces) pineapple chunks or tidbits
- 5 cups cooked kernel corn, fresh or canned
- 1 teaspoon paprika
- ¼ cup sour cream
- 2 tablespoons water
- 2 teaspoons cornstarch

In skillet, mix frankfurters with onions, garlic, tomato sauce, pineapple juice, green peppers and pineapple.

Cover and simmer 5 minutes; add corn and paprika; cover and simmer 10 minutes.

Meanwhile, blend sour cream with water and cornstarch until smooth and free from lumps. Add to foods in skillet; cook, stirring constantly, until mixture comes to boil. Remove from heat.

Serve with Italian or French bread and a generous bowl of crisp salad greens with French dressing.

Stuffed Hot Dogs

Total Time: about 20 minutes   Serves: 6

  12 skinless frankfurters
   Applesauce
   Mustard
  12 slices bacon (optional)

Sauté frankfurters on well-oiled griddle for 5 minutes, turning often. Remove and slit. Fill centers with (canned) applesauce seasoned with mustard. Serve at once.

OR

Slit frankfurters; fill lightly with seasoned applesauce as above; wrap in bacon strips and broil as above, turning frequently until bacon is crisp. Serve at once. Serve with potato or corn chips and dill pickles.

Hungry Boy Flapjacks

Total Time: about 20 minutes   Serves: 6

   Basic pancake batter
  12 skinless frankfurters
   Catsup
   Mustard
   Pickle relish

Prepare pancake batter according to package directions. Slice frankfurters ¼ inch thick in penny shapes. Add to batter. Prepare pancakes on hot griddle as usual. Serve piping hot with catsup, mustard, and pickle relish; or with canned (drained) asparagus and potato chips.

Broiled Hash 'n' Eggs

Total Time: about 15 minutes   Serves: 4

    3 tablespoons butter or margarine
 ½ cup chopped onions
 ¼ teaspoon dried marjoram
    1 can (1 pound) corned beef, cut up
    2 medium-sized boiled potatoes, chopped
    4 eggs

In large skillet with oven-proof handle, melt butter and
sauté onions until glazy, about 3 minutes. Add marjoram,
corned beef and potatoes; blend well.

In top of hash, make four hollows with bowl of spoon
and drop eggs into the "nests."

Preheat broiler to 350° F. Place skillet on rack in broiler
oven and broil 4 inches below source of heat until eggs are
set, 3 to 4 minutes. Serve at once with tangy cole slaw in
separate dish.

Quick Beef Scramble

Total Time: about 15 minutes   Serves: 4 to 6

    2 tablespoons olive or salad oil
    1 jar (2½ ounces) sliced dried beef
    1 can (10½ ounces) condensed cream of celery
         soup, undiluted
 ½ cup red or white wine
    1 cup shredded American cheese, about ¼ pound
    2 to 3 tablespoons chopped ripe olives
 ¼ cup chopped (canned) pimientos
    1 tablespoon minced parsley or chives

If dried beef is very salty, cover with boiling water for
2 minutes; drain well before using.

In heavy skillet, heat oil. Add beef and sauté until edges curl. Mix soup with wine; add to beef mixture. Cook until creamy and smooth, stirring constantly. Mix in cheese, olives and pimientos. Reduce heat; cook until cheese is melted, about 3 minutes.

Serve at once with buttered kernel corn or hot biscuits.

Beef à la King

Total Time: about 20 minutes   Serves: 4 to 6

- ¼ pound sliced dried beef, blanched
- 3 tablespoons butter or margarine
- 1 chopped (canned) pimiento
- 3 tablespoons flour
- 1¼ cups milk
- ¼ cup sherry
- 1 can (4 ounces) mushroom stems and pieces

Pull blanched beef into small pieces. In heavy skillet, heat butter; sauté beef until edges curl and meat starts to crisp, about 5 minutes. Blend in pimiento.

Stir in flour and sauté over low heat until flour begins to brown. Add milk, sherry and mushrooms. Stir until gravy thickens and comes to boil. Remove from heat. Serve at once on bed of hot steamed rice or on toast triangles.

VARIETY MEATS

They are rightly called nature's storehouse of vitamins and minerals, and yet they are often neglected in meal planning. Except for sweetbreads and calf's liver, which are considered great delicacies, all variety meats are moderate to low in cost.

How to Plan Variety Meat Servings

Three-fourths to 1 pound equals about four average servings.

How to Store Variety Meats

See *Meat Storage in Transit*. Brains and sweetbreads, if not used immediately, must be precooked and served within 24 hours. Tripe is usually already cooked when purchased; if not, it must be precooked.

How to Cook Variety Meats

Except for pickled, corned, or smoked tongue, all variety meats may be braised. Liver, tripe, sweetbreads, and brains may also be broiled or sautéed.

LIVER

Beef, pork, lamb, and veal liver are all very, very rich in vitamins and minerals. Pork liver, the richest of all, is lowest in cost.

The outer membrane should always be peeled or trimmed off before cooking. Beef and pork liver are best when braised. Lamb and veal liver may be braised, broiled, or sautéed.

To braise sliced liver: Dredge lightly with flour. Brown in lard or bacon drippings. Add desired seasonings, diced or sliced vegetables and ½ cup liquid. Cover cooker tightly and braise over low heat until tender, about 20 to 30 minutes.

To broil: Dip ½ to ¾-inch-thick slices in melted bacon drippings or butter. Broil at moderate temperature, approximately 3 inches from source of heat, for about 8 to 10 minutes; turn once.

To sauté: Roll ½ to ¾-inch-thick slices in flour. Sauté in a small amount of bacon drippings or lard over low heat until fork-tender.

Liver Loaf

Total Time: about 1 hour   Serves: 6

    1 pound sliced beef or lamb liver
    3 strips bacon
 ½ cup chopped onions
    2 stalks celery with leaves, cut up
    2 eggs, slightly beaten
    1 cup soft bread crumbs
    1 teaspoon salt
 ¼ teaspoon dried thyme
 ⅛ teaspoon black pepper
 ½ cup milk or tomato juice
Optional:
    3 bacon strips

Simmer liver in water to cover for 2 minutes; drain. In skillet, sauté bacon until crisp; remove and reserve. In bacon fat, sauté onion and celery for 5 minutes; stir occasionally.

In food chopper or electric blender, grind together liver, bacon and the sautéed vegetables. Mix with remaining ingredients except bacon strips.

Turn into a greased (1-quart) loaf pan. Brush surface with bacon drippings or cover with additional strips of bacon.

Bake in a moderate (350° F.) oven for about 45 minutes. Turn out on preheated platter. Serve with tomato or onion sauce and lettuce cups.

Austrian Liver Sauté

Total Time: about 25 minutes   Serves: 4

- 1 pound sliced beef or calf's liver,
     cut in 1-inch squares
- 2 to 4 tablespoons flour
- ¼ cup butter or margarine
- ½ cup chopped onions
- 1 teaspoon drained capers, chopped
- ½ teaspoon salt
- ½ teaspoon vinegar or white wine
- ¼ teaspoon white pepper
- ¼ teaspoon Hungarian paprika
- ½ cup sour cream

Dip only one side of liver squares in flour; shake off excess. In heavy skillet, heat butter; sauté liver, flour side down, about 3 minutes; turn with tongs and sauté 2 minutes; remove to preheated platter; keep hot.

In drippings left in skillet, sauté onions until golden. Stir in remaining flour mixed with 2 tablespoons cold water for each tablespoon flour; bring to boil, stirring constantly.

Add remaining ingredients except sour cream; blend well. Cover and simmer over low heat for 5 minutes.

Blend in sour cream; stir until thoroughly heated but do not boil. Add liver to reheat, if necessary.

Serve at once on bed of steamed rice. Serve with tomato slices in French or Russian dressing.

Liver Barbecue

Total Time: about 45 minutes,   Serves: 4
including marinating

   1 pound sliced beef or calf's liver,
      cut in 4 servings
   Quick Barbecue Sauce recipe

Marinate liver in Barbecue Sauce for 30 minutes. Line
broiler pan with foil; do not use wire grill. Set oven regulator for broiling. Preheat broiler for 10 minutes.

Place sliced liver in broiler pan; brush with sauce. Broil
3 inches below source of heat for 4 to 5 minutes. Turn liver
pieces with pancake turner; brush with sauce. Broil until
liver is fork-tender, about 5 minutes.

Serve at once on bed of hot steamed spinach or fluffy
mashed potatoes, with remaining hot Barbecue Sauce in
separate dish.

Quick Barbecue Sauce (Cooked)

Total Time: about 5 minutes   Yield: about 1¼ cups sauce

In saucepan, heat ¼ cup butter or margarine; add 1 cup
catsup and 2 tablespoons Worcestershire sauce; bring to
boil. Season to taste with 1 or 2 tablespoons mild vinegar
or diluted lemon juice. Remove from heat. *NOTE:* If a
milder sauce is desired, use only 1 tablespoon Worcestershire sauce.

Hungarian Liver Pörkölt
(Liver Goulash)

Total Time: about 45 minutes   Serves: 4 to 5

  1 pound sliced beef liver, cut in
     ½-inch strips
   Flour
  ¼ cup butter or lard
  ¾ cup chopped onions
  ½ cup beef bouillon or red wine
  1 teaspoon salt
  1 tablespoon Hungarian paprika
  ½ cup sour cream

Roll liver strips in flour. Heat butter in skillet; add liver and onions; sauté for 3 minutes, stirring constantly. Add bouillon, salt and paprika. Cover and simmer over low heat until liver is tender, about 30 minutes.

Shortly before serving, stir sour cream into pan juices; reheat but do not boil. Serve on bed of hot mashed potatoes with tossed salad greens or dill pickles.

BRAINS ★

The brains of beef, lamb, pork and veal are all tender and mild in flavor. Calves' brains are the most popular.

To precook: In large skillet, cover brains with cold water. Add 1 tablespoon lemon juice and 1 teaspoon salt for each quart water. If desired, add one onion studded with two whole cloves, one bay leaf and a parsley sprig.

Bring liquid to boil. Reduce heat immediately. Cover and simmer for about 20 minutes. Remove membranes with tip of a paring knife.

To serve: Precooked brains may be cut into small pieces and scrambled with eggs; sliced and reheated in a rich tangy sauce; sliced and fried in a small amount of fat; or dipped in melted butter or margarine before broiling.

Brain Schnitzels ★

Total Time: about 20 minutes   Serves: 4

     2 precooked calves' brains,
          cut in ¼-inch slices
     Flour
     Salt and white pepper
     1 egg
     1 tablespoon water
     Dry bread crumbs
     ½ cup butter or margarine
     Lemon slices

Dip brain slices in seasoned flour, then in egg mixed with water, and finally in bread crumbs. Sauté schnitzels in hot butter until brown, about 10 minutes, turning once or twice with pancake turner. Garnish with lemon slices. Serve at once with creamed spinach and broiled tomato halves sprinkled with grated cheese.

Baked Brains ★

Total Time: about 25 minutes   Serves: 4 to 5

     1 pound precooked brains, diced
     1 cup plain yogurt
     3 eggs, well beaten
     2 tablespoons flour
     ¼ teaspoon salt
     ⅛ teaspoon white pepper

Place diced brains in a shallow, well-oiled casserole. Blend yogurt with remaining ingredients and spread over brains. Bake in a moderate (350° F.) oven until lightly browned and well heated, about 15 to 20 minutes. Serve at once with mixed vegetables or Turkish Pilaf; see *Index*.

HEART ★

Wash and remove hard parts of the heart before slow braising or simmering.

To simmer: In large saucepan, cover heart with cold water. Add 1 teaspoon salt for each quart water. Bring to boil. Reduce heat. Cover cooker tightly and simmer until tender.

Simmering Time for Heart

Beef	3–3½ hrs.
Lamb, pork, veal	about 2½ hrs.

To braise: Leave whole or slice across grain. In large skillet, heat a small amount of lard or bacon drippings. Brown meat on all sides, about 10 minutes. Add ½ cup liquid. Season to taste. Cover cooker tightly. Braise over low heat until fork-tender. Cooking time is about the same as for simmering; braise sliced beef heart for 1½ to 2 hours.

Hearts may be stuffed before braising.

Heart Fricassee ★

Total Time: about 2 hours   Serves: 4

- 1 pound veal or lamb hearts
  Flour
- ¼ cup lard or bacon drippings
- ½ cup chopped onion
- 1 teaspoon salt
- ¼ teaspoon celery seeds
- ⅛ teaspoon dry mustard
- ½ cup red wine
- 1 cup tomato sauce

Wash hearts and remove hard parts. Slice across the grain. Dredge with flour.

In large skillet, heat lard. Add meat and onion; sauté for 10 minutes, turning frequently. Season with salt, celery seeds and mustard. Add wine and tomato sauce; blend.

Cover tightly. Braise over low heat until meat is fork-tender, about 1½ to 2 hours.

Serve with steamed rice and lima beans.

KIDNEYS

Beef, lamb, pork and veal kidneys may be braised. With the exception of beef, all kidneys are tender enough to broil.

To prepare for cooking: Wash very well in cold water and rinse. Beef kidneys are best soaked in cold water for 1 hour. Remove membrane and hard parts. Slice if desired. Lamb kidneys are usually cut in half or left whole.

To braise: Prepare kidneys for cooking. Roll in seasoned flour. In large skillet, heat lard or bacon drippings. Brown kidneys. Add seasonings and liquid: about ¾ cup for beef and ½ cup for all other kidneys. Cover skillet tightly. Braise over low heat until tender.

Braising Time for Kidneys

	TIME
Lamb kidneys	¾–1 hr.
Pork & veal kidneys	1–1½ hrs.
Beef kidneys	1½–2 hrs.

To broil: Prepare kidneys for cooking. Marinate for 1 hour in oil, French dressing or tomato juice. Brush with marinade or melted butter or margarine. Broil about 10 to 12 minutes, turning once.

Kidney Stew

Total Time: about 45 minutes   Serves: 4

      4 veal kidneys
    ¼ cup flour
      2 tablespoons butter or margarine
    ¼ cup chopped onion
    ½ teaspoon salt
    ¼ teaspoon black pepper
      Pinch of grated nutmeg
    ½ cup white wine or chicken bouillon
      1 tablespoon minced parsley

Prepare kidneys for cooking; slice. Dredge with flour.
In large heavy skillet, heat butter. Add kidneys and onion; sauté for 10 minutes, turning often to brown evenly. Add remaining ingredients except parsley; blend well.

Cover tightly. Braise over low heat until kidneys are fork-tender, about 30 minutes. Sprinkle with parsley. Serve piping hot on steamed brown rice with stewed tomatoes in separate dish.

SWEETBREADS ★

The sweetbreads of veal, young beef and lamb have two different parts, sold separately or as a pair: heart and throat. Delicate veal sweetbreads are by far the most popular.

To precook: In large skillet, cover washed sweetbreads with cold water. Add 1 teaspoon salt, 1 tablespoon lemon juice or vinegar and any additional seasoning to each quart of water. Lemon juice helps to keep the meat white and firm. Simmer for 15 to 20 minutes. Rinse and remove membrane and connective tissue with knife.

To braise without precooking: Wash and remove membrane. Dredge with flour and sauté in small amount of fat for about 10 minutes. Add ½ to ¾ cup liquid. Cover and cook over low heat until done, 15 to 20 minutes.

To fry without precooking: Split crosswise if desired. Prepare as for braised. Do not add liquid. Do not cover.

Fry until done, about 20 minutes. Turn occasionally.

To serve: Precooked sweetbreads may be cut into small pieces and scrambled with eggs; reheated in a rich sauce; dipped in egg and crumbs and fried in a small amount of fat or dipped in melted butter or margarine and broiled.

Braised Sweetbreads

Total Time: about 30 minutes   Serves: 4

       1 pound sweetbreads
      ¼ cup butter or margarine
      ¼ cup chopped shallots or 2 tablespoons
          finely chopped onion
      ½ teaspoon salt
      ¼ teaspoon white pepper
      ½ cup sherry or red wine
      ½ cup chicken bouillon
    1½ teaspoons cornstarch
       1 tablespoon water
       1 can (4 ounces) mushroom stems and pieces,
          drained
       2 canned pimientos, chopped
       8 toast triangles
       4 parsley sprigs

Wash sweetbreads and remove membrane. In large skillet, heat butter; sauté sweetbreads and shallots very lightly, about 3 minutes; season with salt and pepper.

Add wine and bouillon. Cover tightly. Braise over low heat for 20 minutes. Remove sweetbreads to hot platter; cut in slices; keep hot.

Blend cornstarch into water until smooth. Stir into meat juices until sauce thickens; add mushrooms and pimientos and heat.

To serve: Place 2 toast triangles on each of four serving platters. Spoon equal quantities of sweetbreads on each platter. Cover with mushroom sauce. Garnish with parsley. Serve at once.

TONGUE ★

Tongue is available fresh, pickled, corned and smoked. Beef and veal tongues are more often available uncooked than those of pork and lamb, which are mostly sold canned and ready to eat.

Smoked and pickled tongues require several hours' soaking in cold water before cooking.

To simmer: In large saucepan or kettle, cover washed tongue with cold water. Add 1 teaspoon salt for each quart liquid when cooking fresh tongue; add spices if desired. Cover cooker tightly and simmer slowly until tender. Plunge into cold water to loosen the skin.

Simmering Time for Fresh Tongue

KIND	HOURS
Beef	3–4
Veal	2–3
Pork	1½–2
Lamb	1–1½

To skin: When tongue is tender, cut off excess fat and hard root end. Slit skin on under side from base to tip. Turn tongue over, with tip end toward you. Carefully slip skin off like a glove.

To slice: Starting at the large end, make thin, even and parallel slices; this will give lengthwise slices from the small end of the tongue.

To serve: If to be served cold, cool tongue in cooking

liquid; it will be juicier. If to be served hot, cool for 15
minutes before slicing. Serve hot or cold with a spicy sauce;
see *Index* for horseradish, raisin, barbecue and cumberland
sauces. Or serve with canned or fresh cranberry sauce,
pickled beets, prepared mustard or horseradish; and
pickles.

Austrian Anchovy Tongue ★

Total Time: about 45 minutes   Serves: 6 or more

    1 medium-size beef tongue, about
      3 pounds, cooked and skinned
    3 tablespoons anchovy paste
    ½ cup butter or margarine
    ¼ cup chopped parsley
    ¼ cup butter or margarine, melted
    Creamed Peas recipe

Cut slightly cooled or cold tongue in diagonal slices
about one-half way through. Blend anchovy paste into
butter at room temperature; mix in parsley. Spread each
tongue slice with anchovy butter. Press slices together;
secure with toothpicks, if necessary.

Place tongue on oiled jelly roll pan; brush with melted
butter. Bake in a moderate (350° F.) oven for ½ hour.
Cut through slices before serving with Creamed Peas.

Creamed Peas

In double boiler over boiling water, heat contents of two
cans (10½ ounces each) of condensed cream of pea soup,
undiluted; season with ¼ cup light or sour cream. Add ½
teaspoon light mustard, if desired.

Smoked Tongue with Raisin Sauce ★

Total Time: about 1¼ hours   Serves: 6 or more

  3 to 4-pound beef tongue, smoked or pickled; cooked
     and skinned
  1 cup seedless raisins
  1 cup prune or apricot juice
  Dash of Worcestershire sauce

Place tongue in shallow roasting pan. Mix raisins, juice
and Worcestershire sauce; pour over tongue. Bake in a
moderate (350° F.) oven for 1 hour, basting frequently.
Serve with boiled potatoes and mixed vegetables.

Sweet-Sour Tongue on Spinach Noodles ★

Total Time: about 25 minutes   Serves: 4 to 6

  Fresh veal tongue, about 1½ pounds, cooked and
     skinned
 ⅓ cup cornstarch
  2 cups apple juice
  2 teaspoons soy sauce
  1 cup light brown sugar
  3 to 4 tablespoons lemon juice or cider vinegar
 ½ tablespoon salt
 ½ teaspoon ginger
 ½ cup chopped green pepper
  4 slices canned pineapple, cut in large pieces
  3 to 4 cups hot spinach noodles

Cut tongue in finger-thick slices; or cube.
In heavy skillet, mix cornstarch with apple juice until
smooth. Add soy sauce, sugar, lemon juice, salt and ginger;

blend well. Bring to boil, stirring constantly. Reduce heat.

Add tongue, green pepper and pineapple; blend again. Cover and simmer over low heat until piping hot, 10 to 15 minutes. The green pepper will be crisp, not soft. Serve on bed of hot spinach noodles.

NOTE: Use equal quantity of beef tongue, if desired. For more tongue recipes, see *Index*.

TRIPE

It may be purchased fresh, pickled or canned. Fresh tripe is usually partially cooked before it is sold; however, it must be cooked in water before it is served. Canned tripe is ready to heat and serve. Pickled tripe is usually thoroughly cooked; it should be soaked before use.

There are two varieties: the plain or smooth and the more popular honeycomb tripe. Their preparation is the same.

To precook: Wash and rinse tripe; place in a large skillet; cover with cold water or equal parts of water and skim milk. Add 1 teaspoon salt for each quart liquid. Cover and simmer until fork-tender, about 1½ hours. Drain and dry between paper towels.

To serve: Cut in serving pieces and heat in a spicy sauce; brush with melted butter or margarine and broil; dip in a batter and fry in deep fat; or serve as an à la king dish.

Catalan Tripe ★

Total Time: about 45 minutes   Serves: 4
1½ hours to precook

  1 pound honeycomb tripe, precooked
  3 tablespoons olive or cooking oil
  3 large tomatoes, chopped
  ½ cup chopped celery, stalks and leaves
  ½ teaspoon salt
  ¼ teaspoon garlic powder
  ⅛ teaspoon onion powder
  ½ cup white wine
    Worcestershire sauce to taste

Cut tripe into strips. Heat oil in large skillet. Lightly
sauté tomatoes and celery for 10 minutes, stirring occasionally. Add tripe, the three seasonings and wine; blend.
Cover and simmer for 25 to 30 minutes. Season with
Worcestershire sauce to taste.

Serve at once with steamed brown rice or boiled potatoes; and a tossed green salad.

3

LEFTOVERS WITH CHARACTER

This chapter is really a cookbook in itself. It presents an entirely new concept, that of serving all types of already-cooked meat in attractive main dishes that are table-ready in little time and at small expense.

Leftovers are no longer an "inevitable" and dreaded end but, rather, the beginning of tasty meals with an altogether different character. With that desirable purpose in mind, many gourmet cooks prepare larger quantities of meat; to them, already-cooked meat is welcome and precious.

No matter how large or small the quantity, leftover meat has an unlimited range of serving possibilities. For example, a denuded ham bone will still add its good flavor to the traditional Boston baked beans.

Leftover cooking is a flexible technique. In your planning, always start with the largest quantity of flavorful meat on hand and go from there to the smaller, and the still smaller, until you finally use the last "bits and pieces" in creative disguise.

There are three distinct parts to *Leftovers with Character*. They are arranged according to what you may have: sliced, cubed or diced, cut up, chopped, minced, or ground cooked meat.

Thirty-Three Ways to Use Leftover Meat will give you a bird's-eye view of what you can do with any leftover meat. Once you have made your selection, refer to *Flavors to Flatter* for seasoning suggestions.

Fingertip Quickies for Leftover Meat gives simple recipes for hearty meals that can be served in less than 30 minutes.

Recipes for Leftovers with Character lists (at the top of each recipe) the kind of cooked meat needed as well as its approximate quantity. In these recipes, you need not measure the meat with an apothecary scale; a little more or less will not alter the good taste of the finished dish.

Since many recipes may be used for several kinds of leftover meat, you have a choice of forty-two different main dishes at your fingertip: in keeping with the book's promise to save you time in the kitchen, twenty-nine dishes will be ready to serve in less than 30 minutes and nine will be ready in 45 minutes. Only four dishes will take an hour.

Look in the *Index* for your favorite leftover dishes.

THIRTY-THREE WAYS TO USE
LEFTOVER MEAT

COOKED MEAT	USE
Sliced	hot or cold sandwiches; heated in barbecue sauce or leftover gravy.

Cubed or
Diced
¾ to 1¼ in.
	in casseroles with:
	    cooked macaroni or spaghetti in a tasty gravy;
	    cooked vegetables in a tasty gravy.
	in a stew;
	in a fried hash;
	in a pie or individual pies;
	in a main dish Chef's Salad.

Cut Up	in creamed, deviled, and curried dishes; served on toast or English muffins.

Chopped	folded into egg dishes: scrambled eggs, omelet, souf-
	    flé, fondue or au gratin;
	as stuffing for green peppers, eggplant, tomatoes, cab-
	    bage rolls, baked potatoes;
	in a spaghetti sauce;
	folded into spaghetti, macaroni, or noodles;
	in a baked hash.

Minced or
Ground
	in croquettes, fritters; mixed with seasoned mashed
	    potatoes;
	in meat loaf;
	sprinkled on creamed soups and vegetables (before
	    serving);
	as a sandwich filling, blended with mayonnaise or
	    salad dressing;
	in a salad dressing (Chef's Salad).

Gravy	add to steamed vegetables; add to egg dishes.
Simmering *Liquid*	use for cooking vegetables (cabbage).
Bones	use for cooking baked beans.

FINGERTIP QUICKIES FOR LEFTOVER MEAT

For sliced cooked meat of any kind:

Breaded Cutlets

Dredge fairly thick slices of cooked meat with flour. Dip in milk and then in well-seasoned dry bread crumbs. Sauté in hot fat or deep-fat fry. Serve with mixed green salad. *1 serving = 1 or 2 cutlets.*

For sliced cooked beef pot roast or pork roast:

Jiffy Barbecue

In fat drippings, brown slices of cooked meat. Add a spicy barbecue sauce (for recipe, see *Index*) and blend. Cover and simmer until heated through. Sprinkle with parsley. Serve with shoestring potatoes or potato chips and pickles. *1 serving = 1 or 2 slices.*

For 4 slices cooked tongue or ham:

Tongue or Ham Divan

In an oiled shallow baking dish or casserole, place 2 cups chopped cooked broccoli (fresh or frozen). Cover with four slices cooked meat. Spread thinly with mayonnaise which has been seasoned with paprika and chopped parsley. Cover with thin slices American cheese or sprinkle with grated Parmesan cheese. Bake in preheated moderate (375° F.) oven for 10 to 15 minutes. *Serves 4.*

For thin, fairly large slices of cooked pork, beef pot roast, or ham:

Cold Roll-Ups ★

Total Time: to prepare, about 15 minutes;
to chill, one hour or overnight

Spread thin slices of cooked meat with a mixture of sour cream, prepared mustard and a few spoonfuls of cooked rice or finely crushed potato or corn chips. Roll up, fasten with toothpicks and chill for at least 1 hour (or overnight) before serving. *1 serving = 1 or 2 rolls.*

For sliced cooked tongue or corned beef:

Frizzle Broil

In hot fat, sauté thin slices of cooked meat. Place on broiler rack. Sprinkle lightly with brown sugar mixed with fat from pan. Broil to glaze, 3 inches below source of heat, about 5 to 8 minutes. Do not turn. Serve at once with fluffy mashed potatoes or mixed vegetables. *1 serving = about 2 slices.*

For sliced cooked meat loaf:

Meat Loaf Surprise

Spread slices of cooked meat loaf with light mustard; place on oiled cooky sheet. Sprinkle slices with finely crushed potato chips and top with a tomato half, cut side down. Bake in a moderate (375° F.) oven until tomatoes are tender and brown, about 15 minutes. Serve with tossed green salad and crusty French bread. *1 serving = about 2 slices.*

For cut-up cooked ham or veal:

Ham or Veal Creole

Measure equal quantities of cut-up cooked meat. Simmer in a spicy Creole sauce containing chopped green pepper, onion, celery, tomato and wine. Serve with steamed brown or white rice. *1 serving = ½ to ¾ cup creole.*

For about 2 cups cut-up cooked pork or ham:

Crusty Pork or Ham Casserole

In a (1½-quart) casserole, mix the contents of one can condensed cream of mushroom or tomato soup with one-half can milk or bouillon. Blend in 2 cups cut-up cooked meat and 1 tablespoon minced parsley. Season to taste with dried marjoram, salt and pepper. Top with about 1 cup crushed potato chips and sprinkle with ¼ to ½ cup water, depending on width of casserole. Bake in a moderate (350° F.) oven for 20 minutes. Serve with lettuce cups in spicy dressing, or tomato wedges. *Serves 4 to 6.*

For about 2 to 3 cups cut-up cooked beef, lamb, pork, ham, or veal:

Spanish Stew

Slice two or three onions; brown lightly in olive oil; season with salt and pepper; add 2 to 3 cups cut-up meat,

1 cup chicken bouillon and ½ cup red wine. Blend well. Bring to boil. Cover and simmer over low heat until piping hot, about 10 to 15 minutes. Serve on bed of steamed rice or a green vegetable. *Serves 4 to 6.*

For cooked ground meat of any kind:

Stuffed Red or Green Peppers

Blend equal quantities of cooked ground meat with cooked rice; season to taste with salt, pepper and paprika. Moisten with milk, bouillon or vegetable juice. Pack lightly into parboiled pepper shells. Bake in a moderate (375° F.) oven until shells are tender, about 25 minutes. Serve with mixed vegetables or cole slaw. *1 serving* = 1 stuffed pepper.

For (ground) cooked meat loaves and patties of any kind:

Stuffed Pancakes

Heat chopped cooked meat in well-seasoned gravy or bouillon. Place spoonfuls in center of large pancakes; roll up to serve with any remaining hot meat in separate dish. Serve with assorted pickles. *1 serving* = 2 or 3 pancakes.

For (ground) cooked meat loaves and patties of any kind:

Stuffed Cabbage

Moisten ground cooked meat with wine, bouillon or milk. Season to taste with marjoram, salt and pepper. Wrap in (parboiled) cabbage leaves and place in casserole. Mix tomato sauce with red wine and add to food in casserole. Bake, uncovered, in a moderate (350° F.) oven about 20 minutes. Serve with home-fried potatoes or potato chips. *1 serving* = 1 or 2 rolls.

Recipes for
LEFTOVERS WITH CHARACTER

For about 6 large or 2 cups smaller slices of cooked beef pot roast or boiled beef:

Miroton of Beef

Total Time: about 45 minutes   Serves: 4 to 6

    2 cups sliced or chopped onions
    2 tablespoons flour
    2 to 3 tablespoons butter or lard
1½ cups hot bouillon
    ½ cup dry white wine
    6 large, or 2 cups small, slices cooked beef
    Salt and pepper to taste
    Minced parsley

Dredge onions with flour. Heat fat in heavy skillet; sauté onions until they begin to brown, stirring constantly, about 10 minutes. Add bouillon and wine; cook until sauce thickens, stirring frequently.

Add meat and blend. Reduce heat. Cover and simmer for about 20 minutes. Season to taste. Sprinkle with parsley before serving with jacket potatoes and buttered sliced or diced carrots.

*For about 3 cups cubed cooked beef pot roast, braised
steak, or stew:*

Red Flannel Hash

Total Time: about 45 minutes   Serves: 6

    3 cups cubed cooked beef
    3 cups chopped cooked potatoes, fresh or canned
 1½ cups finely chopped cooked beets, fresh or canned
  ⅛ teaspoon salt
  ⅛ teaspoon black pepper
  ⅛ teaspoon dried marjoram
  ¼ cup milk or light cream (or more)
    4 tablespoons bacon drippings or oil

In large bowl, blend first six ingredients in order given.
Add enough milk to moisten; blend again.

Melt fat in heavy skillet; add meat mixture and press
down evenly with spatula. Cook over medium heat until
crisp and golden brown on bottom, 5 to 10 minutes.

Fold over like an omelet; press down lightly. Reduce
heat again and cook until hash can be turned out on a
preheated platter, 20 to 25 minutes. Serve with a tossed
green salad with Italian or Russian dressing.

For about 3 cups chopped cooked beef pot roast or stew:

Stuffed Green Peppers

Total Time: about 1 hour   Serves: 6

6 medium green peppers
3 cups chopped cooked beef
¼ cup chopped onions
¼ cup celery stalks
2 teaspoons salt
¼ teaspoon paprika
2 (or slightly more) cups cooked rice
2 cups tomato juice
1 teaspoon lemon juice
¼ teaspoon salt
¼ teaspoon celery seeds

Wash peppers; cut a thin slice from stem ends; remove seeds. Parboil peppers and drain. Place in shallow baking dish large enough to hold peppers straight.

Meanwhile, blend meat with onion, celery, salt and paprika. Add enough rice for stuffing the peppers; blend. With large spoon, stuff peppers; do not pack too tightly.

Blend tomato juice with the three seasonings and pour over peppers.

Bake in a moderate (350° F.) oven until peppers are tender, 35 to 45 minutes depending on the size of the vegetable. Serve with dilled cucumber salad.

NOTE: If desired, pour 1 cup water into baking dish before baking.

For about 3 cups minced or ground cooked beef:

German Beef-Potato Casserole

Total Time: about 45 minutes   Serves: 6

- 3 cups minced or ground cooked beef
- ½ cup chopped onion
- 1 clove garlic, minced or puréed
- 1 cup beef or chicken bouillon or leftover gravy
- ½ cup red wine
- ½ teaspoon Worcestershire sauce
- 3 cups prepared instant mashed potatoes, well seasoned
- 1 tablespoon minced parsley or chives

In skillet or casserole, blend meat with onion, garlic, bouillon, wine and Worcestershire sauce; heat over low flame; remove and reserve.

Place one-half of mashed potatoes in skillet; cover with hot meat mixture and arrange remaining potatoes in a circle close to outer rim of casserole.

Bake in a moderate (350° F.) oven until mixture is heated through and potatoes are lightly browned, about 30 minutes. Sprinkle center with parsley and serve with mixed vegetables.

For about 2 cups chopped cooked beef pot roast or stew:

Southern Beef Hash

Total Time: about 30 minutes   Serves: 4 to 6

   2 cups chopped cooked beef
   3 cups chopped cooked potatoes, fresh or canned
   ½ cup leftover or canned gravy
   ½ teaspoon salt
   ¼ teaspoon black pepper
   ¼ teaspoon garlic powder
   2 eggs, beaten
   ¼ cup lard, butter or margarine
   Chopped pickles

In large bowl, mix the first seven ingredients in order given.

In large skillet, heat fat. Add meat mixture and spread evenly over bottom with the back of a spoon.

Cook slowly over low heat until browned on bottom, about 20 to 25 minutes.

To serve: Fold like an omelet and slide onto a pre-heated platter. Sprinkle with chopped pickle. Serve with buttered squash and cole slaw.

For about 2 cups chopped cooked (or canned) corned beef; also smoked pork and tongue:

Old-Fashioned Hash

Total Time: about 45 minutes   Serves: 4 or more

   2 cups chopped cooked or canned corned beef
   2 cups chopped cooked potatoes, fresh or canned
   ¾ cup chopped onions
   ¼ teaspoon salt
   ⅛ teaspoon black pepper
   3 to 4 tablespoons bacon drippings or fat
   Parsley or watercress sprigs

In large bowl, blend meat with vegetables and seasonings.

In heavy skillet, heat fat; add meat mixture and press down evenly with spatula. Cook slowly over low heat until a brown crust forms on bottom, about 20 to 30 minutes.

To serve: Fold like an omelet and slide onto a preheated platter. Garnish with parsley and serve at once with pickles and steamed sweet-sour beets.

For about 2 cups cut-up cooked lamb:

Lamb Stroganoff

Total Time: about 25 minutes   Serves: 6

    2 cups cut-up cooked lamb
  ½ pound broad egg noodles
    4 tablespoons butter or margarine
  ½ cup chopped onions
  ½ cup sliced mushrooms, fresh or canned
  ½ teaspoon salt
  ¼ teaspoon black or white pepper
    Pinch of nutmeg
    1 cup sour cream
    Pimiento strips

Cut lamb in ½-inch julienne strips. Cook noodles as package directs; drain and keep hot.

In heavy skillet, heat butter. Add onions and mushrooms; sauté until onions are golden, stirring frequently, about 10 minutes.

Add meat and brown on all sides, about 5 minutes. Season with salt, pepper and nutmeg. Stir in sour cream; reheat if necessary.

Serve on bed of hot noodles. Garnish with pimiento strips. Serve with a mixed vegetable salad.

For about 2 cups cut-up cooked lamb or veal:

Shepherd's Pie

Total Time: about 30 minutes   Serves: 6

    2 tablespoons butter or margarine
    2 tablespoons minced onion
    1 clove garlic, mashed or puréed
    ¾ cup thinly sliced celery
    2 cups cut-up cooked meat
    2 cups leftover or canned gravy
    2 tablespoons sherry (optional)
    ¼ cup chopped parsley
    ½ teaspoon salt
    ⅛ teaspoon black or white pepper
    3 egg yolks, beaten
    3 cups hot mashed potatoes

Preheat oven to 425° F.

In (1½-quart) casserole, heat butter. Sauté onion, garlic and celery, stirring frequently, for 5 minutes.

Add meat, gravy, sherry, parsley, salt and pepper; blend and simmer over low heat for about 5 minutes.

Add egg yolks to mashed potatoes and beat well. Arrange in ring form on top of meat; press down lightly with back of spoon.

Bake in a hot (425° F.) oven until potatoes are light brown, 10 to 15 minutes. Serve piping hot with a mixed vegetable salad.

For about 2 cups cut-up cooked lamb or veal:

Mandarin Curry

Total Time: about 20 minutes   Serves: 4 or more

 3 tablespoons butter or margarine
 2 tablespoons brown sugar
 3 cups leftover or canned gravy
 2 cups cut-up cooked meat
 1 can (11 ounces) mandarin orange segments, drained
 1 teaspoon curry powder
 ½ teaspoon salt
 ¼ teaspoon white pepper
 3 to 4 cups hot steamed rice
 Chopped parsley
 Paprika
 Quick Curry Sauce recipe

In heavy skillet, heat butter and sugar; stir until sugar is dissolved. Add gravy, meat, orange segments and the three seasonings; blend. Cover and simmer over low heat until thoroughly heated, 10 to 15 minutes.

Arrange cooked rice in ring on preheated platter. Turn curry into center of ring. Sprinkle generously with parsley and dust with paprika. Serve sauce in separate dish.

NOTE: To make about 4 cups rice, use either 1½ cups regular or 2 cups packaged precooked rice.

Quick Curry Sauce ★

Total Time: about 5 minutes   Yield: about 1 cup

Chop ¼ to ⅓ cup bottled chutney; blend with 1 teaspoon curry powder and 1 cup of either sour cream, heavy cream or chilled evaporated milk. Chill before use.

For 1½ cups chopped cooked lamb or veal:

Stuffed Italian-Style Tomatoes

Total Time: about 30 minutes   Serves: 6

         6 large tomatoes
      1½ cups soft bread crumbs
         3 chopped anchovy fillets
      1½ tablespoons drained (bottled) capers
      1½ cups chopped cooked meat
        ¼ cup light cream
         1 tablespoon Marsala wine or sherry (optional)
         1 tablespoon olive or salad oil
         6 slices buttered toast
         6 pickles, cut into fans
         6 radish roses

Scoop out centers of tomatoes; reserve for future use. Turn tomatoes upside down on rack to drain.

Combine bread crumbs, anchovy, capers, meat, cream and wine. Fill tomatoes with mixture; sprinkle with oil.

Bake in a moderate (350° F.) oven for 20 minutes.

Cut toast slices crosswise into triangles; arrange tomatoes in center of six individual plates; surround with toast triangles, pickle fans, and radish roses (see *Eatable Garnishes*).

For about 2 cups sliced cooked lean fresh pork:

Jachtschotel
(A Dutch Pork Casserole
with Green Apples)

Total Time: about 1 hour   Serves: 6 to 8

      6 tablespoons butter or margarine
      1 large onion, sliced
      3 to 4 green apples, sliced ¼ inch thick
      2 cups sliced cooked potatoes, fresh or canned
      2 cups sliced cooked (lean) fresh pork
    2½ cups leftover or canned gravy
      1 teaspoon salt
      ¼ teaspoon white pepper
      ⅛ teaspoon nutmeg
      ½ cup dry bread crumbs (optional)

In a (2-quart) casserole, melt 2 tablespoons butter; add onion rings and sauté until golden brown, about 5 minutes; remove and reserve.

In same casserole, melt remaining 4 tablespoons butter; add apple slices and sauté 5 minutes; remove and reserve.

Place 1 cup sliced potatoes in bottom of casserole; cover with meat, then with onions, then with apples and finally with remaining 1 cup sliced potatoes; spread each layer evenly.

Season gravy with salt, pepper and nutmeg; pour over mixture in casserole. Sprinkle with bread crumbs.

Bake in a moderate (350° F.) oven for 45 minutes. Serve with steamed baby carrots and green peas.

For about 3 cups cubed cooked pork:

Pork Curry

Total Time: about 40 minutes   Serves: 6

   ¼ cup oil
   ½ cup finely chopped onions
   ½ cup chopped celery
   1 clove garlic, minced or puréed
   1 small apple, peeled and diced
   ⅓ cup flour
   2 cups bouillon
   ½ teaspoon salt
   1 tablespoon curry powder
   3 cups cubed cooked pork
   3 to 4 cups steamed rice

Curry Accompaniments:

chopped hard-cooked egg yolks
chopped hard-cooked egg whites
shredded moist coconut
seedless raisins
pineapple tidbits
chutney
peanuts

In heavy skillet, heat oil; add onion, celery, garlic and apple; sauté until soft, about 10 minutes. Stir often.

Stir in flour; slowly add bouillon; cook and stir until sauce is thickened, about 10 minutes. Season with salt and curry powder.

Add pork; blend again. Cover and simmer over low heat for 15 minutes. Serve over hot steamed rice. The accompaniments are served separately in small bowls.

For about 3 cups cut-up cooked pork:

Pork Chow Mein

Total Time: about 25 minutes   Serves: 6

 3 cups cut-up cooked pork
 2 cups leftover or canned gravy
 1 cup finely chopped green pepper
 2 cups pineapple chunks
 2 to 3 tablespoons soy sauce
 1 can (1 pound) bean sprouts, drained and rinsed
 1 cup pineapple juice (from chunks)
 2 to 3 tablespoons cornstarch
 Canned chow mein noodles

In skillet, heat meat in gravy with green pepper and
pineapple. Add soy sauce to taste; blend in bean sprouts.
Measure ½ cup liquid from skillet and add pineapple
juice; mix with cornstarch and return to skillet; cook until
smooth and slightly thickened, about 5 minutes.
Serve on preheated platter on bed of chow mein noodles.
Serve steamed rice in separate dish.

For about 2 cups chopped cooked pork, ham, or beef:

Western Omelet

Total Time: about 30 minutes   Serves: 4

 2 tablespoons butter or margarine
 ¾ cup chopped onion
 ½ cup chopped green pepper
 2 cups chopped cooked meat
 4 eggs, beaten
 3 tablespoons milk or cream
 ½ teaspoon salt
 ¼ teaspoon black pepper
 ⅛ teaspoon paprika
 Minced parsley or chives

In heavy skillet, melt butter; add onion and green pepper. Sauté until soft and transparent, about 5 minutes, stirring frequently. Add chopped meat and sauté 5 to 8 minutes, stirring often.

Meanwhile, blend eggs with milk, salt, pepper and paprika. Pour over mixture in skillet and cook until firm. Turn over and cook until underside is lightly browned. Sprinkle with parsley.

Serve at once, with toast triangles, cole slaw, and pickles.

For about 1 cup chopped cooked fresh pork:

Chinese Eggs Foo Young

Total Time: about 25 minutes   Serves: 4 to 6

    1 cup chopped cooked fresh pork
    1 can (1 pound) bean sprouts, drained and rinsed
    ½ cup thinly sliced onions or scallions
    6 eggs, well beaten
    ½ cup bacon drippings or oil
    Hot Soy Sauce recipe

In bowl, mix pork with bean sprouts and onions; blend in eggs.

In large skillet or griddle, heat fat. Drop 2 tablespoons of meat mixture at a time into hot fat. Fry like pancakes until brown. Turn carefully with pancake turner to brown second side; remove to hot platter and keep hot until all the mixture is cooked. Arrange on hot platter. Cover with hot sauce or serve sauce in separate pitcher. *NOTE:* You may want to cook the Soy Sauce in advance and reheat before serving.

Hot Soy Sauce ★

In saucepan, heat 2 cups chicken bouillon. Blend 2 tablespoons cornstarch with 2 tablespoons soy sauce; stir into ½ cup hot bouillon. Slowly stir into the remaining bouillon until free from lumps and slightly thickened. Season to taste with salt and white pepper. Yield: about 2 cups sauce.

For about 3 cups diced cooked ham:

Ham Jambalaya

Total Time: about 45 minutes   Serves: 6

- 3 slices bacon, chopped
- 3 scallions, tops and bulbs chopped; or ¼ cup chopped onion
- ¾ cup chopped green pepper
- 1 clove garlic, minced or puréed
- 3½ cups tomatoes, cooked or canned
- ½ cup dry white wine
- ½ teaspoon salt
- ½ teaspoon dried thyme
- ¼ teaspoon dried basil
- ¼ teaspoon dried marjoram
- ¼ teaspoon paprika
- ¼ teaspoon Tabasco
- 2 cups diced cooked ham
- 1 cup uncooked regular rice
- 1 tablespoon chopped parsley or chives

In heavy skillet or casserole, sauté bacon, scallions, green pepper, and garlic until tender, about 10 minutes, stirring frequently. Add tomatoes, wine and the six seasonings; blend well.

Bring mixture to boil; add ham, then add rice gradually, stirring constantly.

Cover tightly; reduce heat and simmer until rice is tender, about 25 minutes. Sprinkle with parsley and serve with cucumber salad in French dressing.

For about 2 cups diced cooked ham or tongue:

Ham or Tongue Chip Mountains

Total Time: about 25 minutes   Serves: 4

    2 cups diced cooked meat
    ½ pound American or Swiss cheese, cubed
    ½ cup mayonnaise or French dressing
    1 teaspoon prepared light mustard
    1 bag (4 or 6 ounces) potato chips
    4 large squares heavy foil

In large bowl, toss meat and cheese. Mix mayonnaise with mustard and blend into meat mixture together with lightly crushed chips. Divide mixture into four servings.

Place on foil squares; wrap loosely yet securely. Bake in a moderate (350° F.) oven for 10 to 15 minutes, to heat and melt cheese slightly.

Serve packets, to be opened at the table, on individual platters. Serve with pickles and marinated tomato slices.

For about 1 cup cut-up or chopped cooked ham:

Creamed Ham 'n' Eggs

Total Time: about 15 minutes   Serves: 4

In saucepan, blend contents of one can (10½ ounces) condensed cream of mushroom or celery soup and one can

(4 ounces) mushroom stems and pieces, including liquid, with 1 cup cut-up or chopped cooked ham. Add four sliced hard-cooked eggs and ¼ teaspoon dried fines herbes or dill weeds.

Heat until mixture starts to bubble, stirring constantly. Add ½ cup sour cream seasoned with ⅛ teaspoon white pepper and a dash of Worcestershire sauce; blend and reheat if necessary.

Serve on bed of steamed spinach or spinach noodles.

For about 3 cups ground cooked ham, smoked pork picnic, or butt:

New England Ham and Apple Pie

Total Time: about 1 hour   Serves: 6 to 8

    3 cups ground cooked meat
    4 cups sliced cooking apples
    ½ cup light brown sugar, firmly packed
    1 teaspoon cinnamon
    1 tablespoon butter or margarine
    2 tablespoons lemon juice
    ½ cup apple cider or juice
    Pastry for Pie Crust; see *Index*

In oiled, shallow (2-quart) casserole, arrange alternate layers of meat and apples, making top layer apples.

Blend sugar and cinnamon; sprinkle over apples; dot with butter; add lemon juice and cider. Cover with foil.

Bake in a moderate (350° F.) oven until apples are barely tender, about 35 minutes. Prepare pie crust.

Cover casserole with pie crust; seal edges. Bake in hot (450° F.) oven for 15 minutes or until crust is brown. Serve immediately, with a large bowl of tossed salad greens.

For about 1½ cups minced or ground cooked ham:

Ham Waffles with Currant Sauce

Total Time: about 25 minutes   Serves: 6

Waffles:
    3 eggs
    1 tablespoon brown sugar
1½ cups minced or ground cooked ham
1½ to 1¾ cups milk
    6 tablespoons melted fat
    2 cups sifted flour
    3 teaspoons baking powder
⅛ teaspoon cloves or mace

Currant Sauce (about 1 cup):
    1 cup currant jelly
    2 tablespoons light corn syrup
    1 teaspoon dry mustard
    1 tablespoon lemon juice

To make waffles: In deep bowl, combine eggs, sugar, ham, milk and fat; add sifted dry ingredients and beat until smooth.

Bake in hot waffle iron; serve with currant sauce in separate dish.

To make currant sauce: In small saucepan, mix jelly, corn syrup and mustard. Place over low heat and cook, stirring constantly, until jelly is melted; season with lemon juice.

*For about 2 cups chopped cooked veal, lamb or beef; and
1 cup chopped cooked ham:*

Swedish Meat Salad
(Kjöt Salat)

Total Time: about 15 minutes   Serves: 4 to 6

  2 cups chopped cooked veal, lamb or beef
  1 cup chopped cooked ham
  3 finely chopped anchovy fillets

Salad dressing:

  6 tablespoons olive or salad oil
  2 tablespoons wine or tarragon vinegar
  ¼ teaspoon dry mustard
  ¼ teaspoon minced parsley
  3 tablespoons heavy cream or tomato purée
    Shredded iceberg lettuce or endive

In salad bowl, toss meat, ham, and anchovy. In separate
bowl, blend salad dressing ingredients and mix well with
rotary beater. Pour over the meats.

Toss lightly and serve on bed of shredded lettuce. Serve
with toasted white bread cut into triangles.

For about 1½ cups sliced cooked fresh or smoked tongue:

Oriental Tongue Salad ★

Total Time: about 15 minutes;   Serves: 6
to chill, 30 minutes

    1½ cups sliced cooked tongue
    ½   cup sliced celery
    ¼   cup sliced stuffed green olives
    ¼   cup sliced ripe (pitted) olives
    1   teaspoon grated onion or onion juice
        Juice of 1 lemon
    ¾   cup plain yogurt
    ¼   cup olive oil
    ½   teaspoon garlic powder
        Shredded iceberg or romaine lettuce

Cut tongue into finger-thick strips. In salad bowl, toss tongue with celery, olives and grated onion. Sprinkle with lemon juice and toss again.

Mix yogurt and oil with garlic powder; blend into meat mixture. Chill before serving on shredded lettuce. Serve with warm crackers or garlic bread.

*For about 2 cups chopped or ground cooked tongue or
ham:*

Stuffed Meat Mousse ★

Total Time: Serves: 6 to 8
on day of serving, about 15 minutes;
on day before, about 1 hour

    1 envelope lemon-flavored gelatin
    1 cup boiling water
    2 tablespoons lemon juice
    1 cup chilled evaporated milk
    2 cups chopped or ground cooked meat
    ½ cup chopped sweet pickles
    ½ cup chopped (canned) pimiento
    ½ cup finely chopped celery
    ½ cup mayonnaise
    1 tablespoon prepared light mustard
    1 tablespoon chopped (bottled) capers (optional)
    2 teaspoons grated onion

Fillings:
    1 pound whole green beans, cooked or canned
    3 raw carrots, cut into long strips
    2 hard-cooked eggs, cut into wedges
    6 to 8 ripe olives
    Parsley sprigs

The day before serving: Sprinkle gelatin over boiling
water; stir until dissolved. Add lemon juice; blend. Chill
until mixture has consistency of unbeaten egg white. Stir
in milk; blend well. Fold in meat, pickles, pimiento and
celery; mix very well. Add mayonnaise mixed with mustard, capers and onion; blend again. Turn into (1½-
quart) ring mold which has been rinsed with cold water.
Cover mold and refrigerate.

Before serving: Unmold on chilled platter. Fill ring with
first green beans and carrot strips, then with egg wedges
and olives. Garnish with parsley sprigs. Serve with oven-
warmed Italian bread.

For about 2 cups minced cooked tongue or smoked pork:

German Meat Salad ★

Total Time: to serve, about 15 minutes;   Serves: 4 to 6
on day before, 25 minutes;
to marinate, overnight

   2 cups diced cooked potatoes, fresh or canned
   ½ cup bouillon
   1 cup finely chopped onions
   ½ cup olive or salad oil
   ¼ to ½ cup cider vinegar, to taste
   ½ tablespoon salt
   ¼ teaspoon black pepper
   ¼ teaspoon dry mustard
   ⅛ teaspoon garlic powder
   2 cups minced cooked meat

to garnish:
   Carrot sticks
   Cherry tomatoes
   Pickles

If fresh potatoes are used, chill. In small saucepan, heat bouillon and cook onions until soft, about 15 minutes. Add to potatoes in a bowl and blend lightly. Add the remaining seven ingredients and toss well. Cover, and refrigerate for at least 2 hours or overnight.

To serve: Let salad stand at room temperature for 10 minutes; toss lightly. Garnish with carrot sticks, tomatoes, and pickles.

For about 2 cups chopped cooked tongue or smoked pork:

Chef's Salad

Total Time: about 15 minutes   Serves: 6

Rub large salad bowl with cut clove of garlic, if desired. Tear enough leaves of well-washed and drained crisp greens (Boston lettuce, escarole, endive and watercress) into bite-size pieces to make about 2 quarts. Spread meat over salad greens. If desired, add avocado and cheese slivers. Have about 2 cups French dressing on hand.

At the table, pour dressing over salad servings to suit personal taste and toss lightly until well coated. Serve with crusty Italian bread.

4

KITCHEN ART

We eat with our eyes long before our mouths touch and taste the food before us. Our enjoyment is greatly enhanced when foods look as appetizing and attractive as they taste. Such pleasant feelings of anticipation and true enjoyment have a powerful influence on the body's readiness to assimilate all vital substances within the foods.

How you serve tasty food is as important as what you serve. The thrifty gourmet, therefore, plans and serves meals with harmonious contrasts of color, texture, and taste.

To be an artist in the kitchen, use *Flavors to Flatter*. Then, for more eye appeal, make finishing touches with *Eatable Garnishes*. *Carving Made Easy* will give you the step-by-step directions for cutting meat into attractive, thin slices. And, to do everything with professional ease, select the basic good tools for all art in the kitchen from *Pots and Pans*.

FLAVORS TO FLATTER

A Novel Meat Seasoning Guide

Subtle seasoning is an art that distinguishes the gourmet from the average cook. Unlock your imagination, and with little experience you will express your personal taste in the kitchen with fragrant herbs and the more robust spices. *The Little Kitchen Dictionary* lists under HERBS and SPICES all those commonly used in meat cookery.

If an herb or a spice is new to you, use it sparingly at first, for it is as easy to overflavor as it is to overcook. One good example is the salt shaker that sprinkles food too lavishly and too often.

To kindle your imagination, the following two seasoning guides give suggestions for the kind of meat you cook and the kind of dish you prepare. They do not indicate flavor combinations, since seasonings always must blend in harmoniously with all other recipe ingredients and never overpower the fine taste of meat itself.

To Season the Meat You Cook:

Beef: basil, bay leaf, cayenne (in moderation), chili powder (for Mexican dishes and barbecue sauces), garlic powder (not garlic salt), marjoram, onion powder (not onion salt), oregano, rosemary, tarragon, thyme.

Ham: whole cloves (for baked ham), whole allspice (for ham steaks and picnics).

Lamb: basil, bay leaf, capers, curry powder, garlic, ginger, marjoram, mint, onion powder (not onion salt), paprika, parsley, white pepper, rosemary, tarragon.

Liver: basil, fines herbes (recipe below), pepper, savory.

Pork: basil, caraway seeds, garlic, rosemary, sage, savory.

Sausage: basil, marjoram, paprika.

Veal: basil, bay leaf, fines herbes (recipe below), mint, thyme.

To Season the Dish You Prepare:

Casseroles: before baking, top with buttered bread crumbs seasoned with paprika, finely chopped parsley, and grated dry cheese.

Chops: Before broiling or braising, sprinkle cinnamon or dill on lamb, parsley and white pepper on pork. After

browning, use lemon juice, tomato juice or dry red
wine on lamb; Worcestershire sauce on pork.

Ground Meat (loaves and burgers): celery seeds, marjoram, dry mustard, prepared mustard for hamburgers,
poultry seasoning, rosemary for lamb loaf, sage for
pork, savory for beef.

Oven Roasts: garlic, dry mustard, rosemary, thyme.

Pot Roasts: before braising, allspice for beef; bay leaf,
caraway seeds for sauerbraten; whole cloves, ginger,
marjoram, oregano, savory, white pepper or rosemary
and thyme for lamb.

Steaks: garlic for beef, oregano for Swiss steaks, ground
nutmeg and ginger for Salisbury steaks.

Stews: basil for beef; bay leaf for lamb; celery seeds, chili
powder for gravy; marjoram, oregano, white pepper,
savory for beef.

Fines Herbes Bag
(Classic French Version)

Chop separately: ½ medium onion, 2 scallions, 2 parsley sprigs, ½ small leek and 1 tablespoon fresh leaf marjoram.

Place mixture in center of a square cheesecloth; tie into
a bag with a long, soft string. Place bag in cooking pot as
recipe directs, with string end tied to handle of cooker.
Remove bag before serving or as recipe directs.

Good Seasonings Other than Herbs and Spices:

Small quantities of wine, beer, ginger ale and vegetable
juices. It is not necessary to use expensive or vintage
wines to flavor meat. Any domestic wine will impart its
bouquet to meat and tenderize it at the same time.

Of course, the alcoholic content of wine or beer has
simmered away long before the dish is ready, and the
meat you serve is free of alcohol.

EATABLE GARNISHES

This is a call to color! Garnishes in contrasting colors make any meat dish more attractive. They lend a personal touch to the meal and express your imagination and good taste.

Depending on occasion and mood, eatable garnishes may be simple, more artistic, or quite festive. Festive garnishes may pinch-hit for other side dishes.

Here, in alphabetical order, are twenty-five eatable garnishes for your choice. Use foods on hand. Place garnishes at the side or on top of the meat, whichever looks better.

Very Simple Garnishes

Hard-cooked egg slices: Overlap three slices, and sprinkle with finely minced parsley or dust with paprika.
Raw mushrooms: Slice on egg slicer and dip in lemon juice.
Curly parsley sprigs: Arrange in bouquet fashion.
Potato chip clusters.
Watercress sprigs.
Carrot sticks: Tie into small bundles with a stem of parsley.

Artistic Garnishes

Carrot curls ★: To make carrot curls, cut strips of carrot lengthwise with vegetable parer. Roll; fasten with picks; crisp in ice water.
Celery hearts or curls.

Cucumber slices: Flute with a fork and top with a teaspoon of cottage cheese.

Hard-cooked egg wedges: Dip in minced parsley and dot with tiny (canned) pimiento bits.

Lemon wedges: Dip into paprika or snipped parsley at the wedge line.

Onion rings: Slice very thin, from white or sweet red onions.

Pitted olives: Green or ripe, spike on short carrot sticks.

Green pepper: Cut into small fingers.

Pickles or gherkins ★: Cut into fans. To make pickle fans, slice small pickles into five or six strips, starting at tip end and cutting almost to stem. Spread slices to form an open fan.

Pineapple cubes: Spike on toothpicks, roll in snipped fresh dill.

Radish roses ★: To make radish roses, cut root from radish; leave stem. Slice sides toward stem to make four petals. Crisp in ice water.

Tomato wedges or cherry tomatoes: Sprinkle with grated dry cheese.

Festive Garnishes

Pot roasts and steaks: small, oven-browned potatoes and asparagus tips tied in green pepper or onion rings.

Roast or braised lamb: small carrots rolled in finely chopped mint or parsley, mashed potato "nests" with spoonfuls of tiny green peas in center; orange peel cups filled with mint jelly or cranberry sauce; other tart fruit (in slices) sprinkled with lemon juice.

Pork roast and picnics: glazed sweet potatoes on orange slices; steamed broccoli flowerets dusted with finely chopped hard-cooked eggs.

Broiled lamb chops: Surround with a ring of tiny green peas; top meat with a broiled mushroom cap; serve mint jelly in paper cups or orange cups (see *Roast or braised lamb*).

Boiled beef or tongue: Remove center of cold (cooked or canned) whole beets; fill with horseradish sauce or cooked peas marinated in French dressing.

Broiled or barbecued beef: String on small wooden skewers pearl onions alternating with cherry tomatoes, ripe olives, and scored, unpeeled cucumber slices or midget gherkins.

All roasts and steaks: small slices of raw apples or mandarin orange marinated in sour cream dressing and placed in tiny lettuce cups; marinated red and white onion rings.

CARVING MADE EASY

A good carving set is essential for even, attractive meat slices. In your selection, look for good-quality steel and a blade that will take and hold a keen, sharp edge. There are three basic types.

1. The standard carving set (for roasts and fowl) consists of a knife with an 8- to 9-inch blade, a fork with a special guard to protect the hand when cutting toward the fork, and a sharpening steel.

2. The steak set consists of a knife with a 6- or 7-inch blade, and a fork with or without guard. It can also be used for smaller roasts and fowl.

3. The roast meat slicer and "carver's helper": consists of a meat slicer with long flexible blade (to cut large thin slices); and a carver's helper with widely spread tines to steady a large roast. This set is often preferred for carving larger roasts.

How to Carve Pot Roasts

The thinner the slices, the more tender the meat will taste.

Boneless meat: Carve with a sharp carving knife, slice meat across the grain.

Rolled meat: Remove cord; place meat on platter, seam side down, and slice.

Bone-in meat: Carve with point of a small carving knife; cut across bones and remove them, if possible. Trim meat off other bones. Slice across muscle of thin roasts. To carve thicker roasts, turn each section on its side.

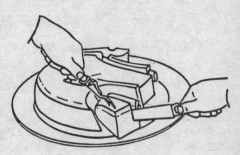

Blade (bone-in) roast

How to Carve Beef Steaks

Braised meat: Slice into serving portions like pot roast.

Broiled meat: Carve across the grain; cut thin diagonal slices in about a 30-degree angle.

Flank Steak: Since it is always broiled rare, it is best placed on a wooden board for carving. Rest for 5 minutes. Then slice across the grain, cutting very thin slices almost parallel to the board.

How to Carve Beef Brisket

Place brisket on platter with the round side away from the carver. Trim off excess fat. Cut thin slices in rotation from three sides, as shown in the illustration. All slices will be across the grain.

Beef brisket

How to Carve Lamb
(after a 10-minute rest)

Unboned Shoulder: It is difficult to carve. Place the roast on a carving board or platter with the round bone to the right. Holding the meat with a carving fork, first cut off the rib bones. Then cut slices from around the round bone. Watch the large flat bone inside the roast. Cut it out very carefully with a sharp small knife. Then slice the meat across the grain.

Boned Rolled Shoulder: Place a longer roast lengthwise on a carving board or serving platter. Holding the meat with a carving fork, carve slices across the grain. Remove each cord only when it is in the way as you cut slices.

Place a smaller roast cut side down on a platter. Holding the meat with a carving fork, slice across the face. As each slice is carved, lift it to the side of the platter or to another hot serving platter.

Cushion Shoulder: Cut slices of desired thickness through the meat and stuffing.

Boned rolled lamb shoulder (small)

Cushion lamb shoulder

How to Carve Pork

Loin Roast: Place on board or platter with bone side up; remove backbone by cutting close along the bone, leaving as much meat on roast as possible. Turn meat side up. Insert carving fork in the top of the roast. Slice close along the side of each rib bone. One slice will have the rib, the next will be boneless.

Pork loin roast

Picnic Shoulder: Carve on wooden board or platter with fat side up and the shank to the carver's right. Anchor meat with carving fork; make a lengthwise basing slice from side opposite elbow bone.

Cut down to arm bone at a point near elbow bone; turn knife and cut along the arm bone to remove the boneless arm meat in one piece.

Slice boneless arm meat across the grain as you slice pot roast.

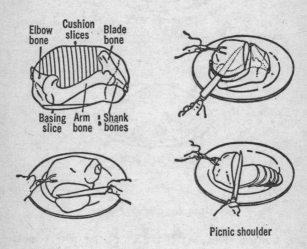

Picnic shoulder

How to Carve Ham

Whole: Place ham on platter with the shank to the carver's right. Cut several slices from the thin (front) side to make a solid base on which to turn the ham.

Turn ham. Starting at the shank end (to the left of the carver), cut a small wedge. Then slice crosswise to the leg bone. To release the slices, cut under them along the bone, starting at the shank end. For additional servings, turn ham over to the original position (as above) and slice.

Center Slices: Divide slice into thirds and turn each sec-

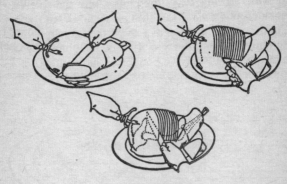

Whole ham

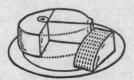

Center ham slices

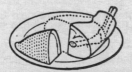

Half ham (shank end)

tion on its largest flat base. Slice across the grain according to thickness desired.

Shank Half: Place ham on platter with the shank to the carver's right. Remove the cushion section (left) and slice, beginning at the large end. For further servings from the remaining section, separate it from the shank by cutting through the joint; remove bone, turn ham and slice.

POTS AND PANS

The well-equipped kitchen is a matter of personal choice and experience rather than of money. Good kitchen equipment is an investment that pays ample dividends in cutting down work and time. It is not the number but, rather, the size and quality of pots and pans that make a kitchen efficient.

The following list is for the fully equipped gourmet meat kitchen. Many of the smaller working tools are available in self-service food markets and five-and-dime stores. Personal choice depends, of course, on the size of your family and kitchen and, to a very great extent, on what kind of cooking you like to do. For instance, if you like pressure-cooking, one pressure pot may not be enough; and if you don't, then you may not need one at all.

Your Personal Helpers:

Portable Timer
Oven mitts
Pot holders
Aprons or smocks
Rubber or disposable kitchen gloves

Paper towels and napkins
Plastic wrap and bags
Aluminum foil (light and heavy)
Garbage bags

For The Top of Your Stove:

All these pots and pans should be of heavy metal with thick bottoms for even heat distribution and tight-fitting regular or self-basting dome covers.

Dutch oven, 4½ to 6 quarts, with rack
Skillets (fry pans), best with oven-proof or removable handles, 6 to 8 inches and 10 to 12 inches wide
Saucepans (pots) in different sizes:
  1 pint
  1 to 1½ quarts
  2 to 2½ quarts
  3 quarts
Casseroles with tight-fitting covers; the kind that take both top-of-stove and oven heat; the freezer-to-table kind are a good investment
Large kettle (8 to 10 quarts) with lid for making soup, spaghetti, etc.
Pressure cooker: 4 or 6-quart, larger size for large meat cuts
Double boiler (best made of glass); top part (if of metal) with rounded bottom makes cleaning easier

For Your Oven:

Standard loaf pans for meat loaves
Glass pie plate(s), 8 or 9 inches in diameter; also handy for watching dumplings cook on top of a stew
Cooling rack
Jelly roll pan for meat loaves, etc.
Oven thermometer (if your oven is without one)
Meat thermometer
Roasting pan with rack
Oven-proof casseroles (see above)

For Table Cooking (if needed):

All electric, with emperature control:

> Table broiler
> Skillet
> Casserole or fryer

Measuring Tools (all standard):

Dry measure cups
  (¼, ⅓, ½ and 1 cup)
Glass measuring cups for liquids
  (1-cup and 1-quart sizes with pouring lip)
Set of metal measuring spoons
  (¼, ½, and 1 teaspoon; 1 tablespoon)

Working Tools

Set of three or four nested mixing bowls
Rotary (egg) beater
Rubber scrapers in different sizes
Wooden spoons
Pan brush with flexible yet sturdy bristles for barbecued
  and broiled meat
Vegetable brush
Spatula (narrow)
Basting spoon or nylon baster
Kitchen tongs
Pancake turner with slots
Deep ladle
Two-tined fork with long handle for barbecuing
Slotted spoon with long handle for barbecuing
Strainer or colander; one large, one small
Sieves of different sizes and mesh thicknesses
Flour sifter
Wire whisk for lumpless gravy

Cheesecloth
Soft cord to tie and truss
Toothpicks (colorless wood)
Chopping and cutting boards: one large, one very small
Egg slicer (also for mushrooms)

Cutlery

Be sure that your cutlery has strong blades that keep sharp when sharpened.

3-inch paring knife
5-inch utility knife
7- or 8-inch chef's knife
    (for chopping, mincing, dicing meat and vegetables)
Carving knife and fork; sharpening steel
Boning knife with (about) 6-inch blade
Vegetable parer with swivel blade
Kitchen shears
Grater or shredder
Skewers: small for the kitchen,
    large for outdoors
Can opener
Bottle opener
Corkscrew
Knife sharpener

Storage Equipment

Four-piece canister set
Containers for refrigeration (at best, the see-through kind)
Freezer wrap
Freezer containers
Freezer tape
Freezer labels

5

KITCHEN SHORTCUTS

Every good cook has a few favorite tricks to save time in the kitchen, but there is always room for a few more. Some of the ones listed here may be familiar, others new.

AT ALL TIMES, have these staples on hand. Depending on your taste, you will use them more or less frequently in the thrift-meat kitchen.

Bouillon cubes, beef and chicken; or instant bouillon packets . . . Butter or margarine . . . Canned foods (creamed soups, gravy, pimiento) . . . Catsup and chili sauce . . . Cheese (grated) . . . Flour . . . Frozen meat vegetables (chopped onions, green peppers, stew vegetables, carrots, potatoes) . . . Herbs and spices . . . Lemon juice (bottled) . . . Mustard . . . Oil . . . Onions . . . Parsley flakes . . . Potatoes (for baking and boiling) . . . Rice . . . Salad dressings . . . Salt and pepper . . . Shortening . . . Tomato juice . . . Vinegar . . . Wine for cooking.

Other favorite staples include: . . . Bacon . . . Capers . . . Eggs . . . Lemons (fresh) . . . Mayonnaise . . . Pasta (macaroni, spaghetti and noodles) . . . Pickles . . . Relishes . . . Tabasco . . . Worcestershire sauce . . . Horseradish (prepared).

Bacon: Baking needs less attention than broiling. Line a pie plate with crumpled foil. Place cold bacon strips on top. Bake in a moderate (350° F.) oven until golden brown, about 10 to 15 minutes, without turning. Bacon will be crisp, with all fat having dripped into the folds of the foil.

Boiled meat: When simmering a large piece of meat, tie with a soft string and attach it to a strong piece of wood (such as a large wooden spoon) placed across the top of the cooker. Meat will cook faster and more evenly.

Bread crumbs: Use one slice of fresh bread for 1 cup

251

soft crumbs or cubes; or one slice of dry or toasted bread for ¾ cup dry cubes or ⅓ cup fine crumbs. To crumble dry bread, put in plastic bag and crush by hand or with soft drink bottle or rolling pin.

Broiler pans: Line with heavy foil to catch drippings and make cleanup quick 'n' easy.

Burgers: For juicier broiled burgers, add 1 tablespoon iced water to each pound of meat before making patties.

Panbroil burgers in heated heavy skillet with about ½ inch of coarse salt instead of fat.

Browning meat cubes: If you crowd the skillet, the meat will steam and not brown. Therefore, sauté meat in smaller batches, moving browned pieces to a hot platter until all browning is done.

Carrots: To skin them easily, drop for a minute in boiling water and remove skin by pulling it with a paring knife.

Cheesecloth: Wring out in cold water and use to wipe meat; strain or drain juices; clean the stove or cutting board; or make a disposable seasoning bag.

Cheese slivers: Use a slit-blade potato peeler instead of a knife.

Chives: Chopped frozen and freeze-dried chives are available in self-service food markets. Add to finished dish shortly before serving; if allowed to cook, chives can "bite."

Defat lamb: Before cooking, cut off as much fat as you can. After browning, drain off accumulated fat.

Defat lamb juices: After roasting, remove meat to pre-heated platter. Set roasting pan in a large shallow pan with iced water. Skim off fat when hardened. Reheat meat juices for serving. For stews, see *Defat Meat Juices*.

Defat meat juices: Wrap large ice cubes in cheesecloth; tie with a long, soft string fastened to a fork. Swish ice cubes back and forth over surface of meat juices. Hardened fat will stick to the cloth and make the lift-off easy. Or quick-cool meat juices as above; skim off fat and reheat for serving.

Diced vegetables: Place vegetable on a wooden board.

With a sharp knife, slice it lengthwise, both horizontally and vertically, in one-half-inch slices. Still holding vegetable, slice again crosswise. Make even slices. Sound complicated? It is really quite easy.

Discard used seasonings: Place garlic, peppercorns, whole cloves, bay leaves, etc., in a small square cheesecloth; tie into a bag with a soft cord long enough to tie to handle of the cooker. Remove bag when recipe directs, without "fishing around" and disturbing the meat.

Dishwashing: Rinse pots and pans in which milk or eggs have been cooked in cool (not hot) water before washing. Wipe greasy dishes with paper towels.

Disposable kitchen gloves are inexpensive . . . cheaper than manicures.

Double boiler: Place a few marbles or pebbles in bottom part of your metal double boiler. They will remind you with jumping bangs when the water gets low.

Dredge meat with flour: How: Plain or seasoned flour put in a shaker jar coats meat well. This process prevents the using of excess flour. *When:* Do it shortly before browning; otherwise meat juices can make the flour soggy.

Dumplings: When steaming them on top of a stew, cover pot with a glass pie plate; watch the dumplings without lifting the cover.

Evaporated milk: Undiluted, it can pinch-hit for cream in most recipes. However, check and correct the seasonings of the finished dish.

Fat removal: See *Defat* . . .

Foods stay warm: When cooked foods must wait, put them (in their cooking pans) in a large roaster; fill roaster halfway with hot water. Cover roaster and keep in a slow (325° F.) oven until ready to serve.

Freeze: Chop onions and green peppers; freeze for later use in individual packages of the amount usually needed. One medium-sized onion equals about ½ cup chopped onion.

Frozen stew vegetables: Self-service food markets carry frozen stew vegetables in small and large bags: chopped onions, chopped green peppers, small and diced or sliced carrots, cut-up stew vegetables, potatoes.

Frozen vegetables: Bake them in the oven while meat is roasting. Remove wrapper and place undefrosted vegetables in heavy foil. Add an ice cube for moisture and a pat or two of butter for seasoning. Close foil tightly. Vegetables will be tender in about 30 minutes; leave unopened in oven if dinner is delayed. Season with salt and pepper before serving.

Gravy without lumps: To thicken about 2 cups of meat juices to a smooth gravy without lumps, pour ¼ cup cold water into a small screw-top (baby food) jar. Sprinkle with 2 tablespoons flour; cover jar and shake vigorously. Add one-half of mixture slowly to hot meat juices. Beat with a wire whisk until gravy comes to a boil. If needed, add remaining flour mixture and beat again until gravy is of desired consistency; simmer for 3 to 5 minutes.

Ground meat: To keep meat from sticking to your fingers, moisten your hands with cold water before shaping patties and meat loaves.

Instant gravy: Thicken meat juices with 1 cup freshly grated carrots or use a tablespoon or two of dehydrated mashed potatoes (packaged mix).

Leftovers: Put in clear containers or plastic wrap for quick identification in the refrigerator.

Lemon juice: For a small quantity, pierce fruit with fork; squeeze out fresh juice drop by drop.

You get more juice out of a lemon if it is heated for 5 minutes in a moderate (350° F.) oven.

Meat juices: To save even the smallest quantity of meat juice for later use, freeze in ice cube tray. Remove frozen cubes to plastic bag and keep frozen until ready to use.

Mince greens: With moistened scissors, cut fresh parsley, chives or mint right onto the food. For larger quantities, rinse greens and shake dry; place in a measuring cup and mince with moistened scissors to desired fineness.

Mixing bowls: To keep them from sliding while you work, place mixing bowls on a damp cloth.

Mushrooms: Clean with a damp cheesecloth. Wash only dirty mushrooms.

To slice, cut off stem end. Run a knife through cap and stem. For uniform slices, press mushrooms gently through egg slicer.

Onions: Peel and cut well chilled, and onions will not make you cry.

To sauté to a golden brown for pot roasts and stews, sprinkle with very little sugar while browning.

To shred, cut a slice from both stem and root ends. Place onion on board, one cut side down; slice vertically and separate into slices.

To make rings, peel onion; hold firmly at stem end and chop downward with a sharp knife, starting at blossom end. Separate slices into rings.

Paper, paper, paper: Use paper towels or napkins to drain bacon and fried foods . . . to dry vegetables . . . to clean a wooden salad bowl and prewipe greasy pots and pans before washing. Use waxed paper on cutting board when you chop or slice and also when you peel, pare, and scrape foods.

Percolator for fat drippings: When no longer good enough to make coffee, use percolator as a container for bacon and other fat drippings; then reheat fat for pouring when needed. Use the coffee basket to strain drippings.

Pork: For an extra-juicy roast or baked ham, baste with ginger ale, club soda, beer or wine once or twice during baking.

Salt: Go easy on salt. When used with herbs and spices, salt easily overpowers their subtle taste.

Be cautious with salt when using bouillon cubes and "instant" mixes, for some products are quite salty. Salt can always be added before serving or at the dinner table.

Sauté in butter: Add a small amount of oil to the butter; butter alone likes to spatter and burn all too easily.

Sour cream: If not at hand when a recipe calls for it, use *chilled* evaporated milk; sour it with 1 tablespoon lemon juice for each cup of (undiluted) milk.

Tomatoes: To peel easily, stroke tomato skin with the dull edge of a knife blade until skin loosens. Or, dip tomato into boiling water for 9 to 12 seconds; cool at once in cold water before peeling.

Toothpicks: (1) Pierce through clove of garlic before adding it to food and discard with ease when no longer wanted in recipe; (2) use toothpick to hold rolled ham or cabbage in shape; (3) pierce through large onions while cooking, and they will not "peel."

6

THE LITTLE KITCHEN DICTIONARY

Arranged in alphabetical order, the following glossary describes the words used in this book.

Aromatic seeds: Commonly used in meat cookery are caraway, celery, dill, mustard and sometimes sesame.

Bake: To cook by dry heat in an oven or oven-type appliance, covered or uncovered. The process of meat cooking in an uncovered casserole, pan or roaster is usually called "roasting." A roasted ham is nevertheless still referred to as "baked."

Barbecue: To roast slowly on a spit, over glowing coals or under a free flame or oven electric unit, usually basting the food with a spicy sauce. Today, the term is also used for meat cooked in or served with a barbecue sauce.

Baste: To moisten meat (or other foods) during cooking; either with its own liquid, fat from the cooker or additional liquids, fats or sauces.

Beat: To mix ingredients with a circular motion, using a rotary or electric beater, a spoon or wire whisk.

Beef: The flesh of mature cattle. Fresh beef is graded for quality and finish.

Blend: To mix two or more foods or recipe ingredients lightly yet thoroughly.

Boil: To heat or cook in a liquid whose temperature reaches 212° F. at sea level.

Bouillon: A clarified stock made from meat, which is delicately seasoned with vegetables, herbs and spices; usually served strained and clear. It can be fresh, canned (concentrated), in cubes or an instant mix. Bouillon cubes are concentrated bouillon shaped into cubes; being dry, they keep well and are convenient to use in cooking. Instant bouillon mix is powdered and readily soluble; it is usually sold in individual packets. Bouillon, broth and consommé are available in various flavors. Follow label directions. Check salt content and reduce salt in recipe if necessary.

Braise: To cook slowly in a tightly covered utensil with a small amount of added liquid and at a very low heat, either on top of stove or in the oven.

Broil: To cook by direct dry heat in a broiler. The food is placed directly under, over or in front of the source of heat or flame. See also: *Panbroil.*

Broth: The soupy liquid in which meat and sometimes vegetables have been cooked. See *Bouillon.*

Brown: To sauté floured or unfloured meat over moderate heat in a small amount of fat to seal in meat juices before braising. The meat is turned frequently for even browning.

Can sizes: Frequently used in meat cookery;

TERM	APPROXIMATE NET WEIGHT OR FLUID MEASURE	CUPS
6 oz.	6 oz.	¾
8 oz.	8 oz.	1
No. 1	11–12 oz.	1⅓–1½
No. 300	14–16 oz.	1¾
No. 303	16–17 oz.	2
No. 2	1 lb. 4 oz.	2½
No. 2½	1 lb. 13 oz.	3½

Casserole: A covered utensil in which food may be cooked and served. As referred to in this book, it is the range and oven-proof casserole which can take both top-of-stove and oven heat.

Chop: To cut into smaller pieces, usually of uniform size, with a sharp knife or chopper.

Consommé: See *Bouillon.*

Cut: Using a sharp knife or scissors, make foods, such as salt pork or green beans, smaller in size.

Dice: To cut into cubes, usually of uniform size.

Dot: To place or sprinkle small quantities of food, such as butter flakes or grated cheese, on the surface of another food.

Dredge: To coat lightly with flour or sprinkle with fine bread crumbs.

Drippings: The fat or juices dripping from meat as it is roasted or broiled; the fat dripping from bacon when cooked; also the natural meat juices accumulating in the cooker when meat is braised. See also: *Meat Juices.*

Dust: To sprinkle lightly with a light substance, such as flour, sugar or spices.

Dutch oven: A deep, heavy-gauge top-of-stove pot with a tight-fitting cover; sometimes with a removable trivet or rack and with two side handles. Its capacity is listed in quarts.

Fell: The thin, paperlike outside covering of lamb. Unless otherwise directed in a recipe, do not remove, as it keeps the meat in shape while cooking. For easier slicing, remove after roasting.

Fry: To cook in hot fat. When the amount of fat is small, it is called "sautéd" or "panfried." When the amount of fat is large, it is called "deep-fat-fried."

Fry pan: See: *Skillet.*

Fricassee: To cook by braising; a term usually used for veal.

Griddle: A shallow, uncovered heavy-gauge utensil with a handle or bail handle. Some griddles have one smooth side for pancakes and fried eggs and another grilled side for chops and burgers. Size is figured by the top outside measurements.

Grill: See *Broil* and *Panbroil.*

Herbs: Unless otherwise stated, all herbs listed in the recipes should be powdered. One tablespoon of a fresh herb is equivalent to 1 teaspoon of the dried (crumbled) or ¼ teaspoon of the powdered herb.

In meat cookery, the most commonly used herbs are: basil, bay leaf, marjoram, mint, oregano, parsley, rosemary, sage, savory, tarragon and thyme. See also: *Spices, Aromatic Seeds* and *Instant Seasonings*.

Instant seasonings: They are powdered celery, celery salt, powdered garlic, garlic salt, powdered onion and onion salt.

Lamb: The flesh of young sheep. Mutton is the flesh of older sheep.

Lard: To insert strips of fat (bacon or salt pork) into uncooked lean meat to add flavor; or to place slices of fat on top of meat before cooking to keep its surface moist.

As a recipe ingredient, lard is rendered pork fat.

Marbling: The fine streaks or flecks of fat running through the lean meat; mostly referred to in beef. The more marbling in meat, the better it tastes and the juicier and more tender it is.

Marinade: A spicy liquid containing vinegar or lemon juice; sometimes also wine. It is used to marinate meat and as a braising and basting liquid.

Marinate: To keep meat in a marinade in order to tenderize the meat and give it additional flavor.

Measure: To measure recipe ingredients with standard measuring cups and spoons. *In this book, all measurements are level.* Weight measure: 16 ounces = 1 pound.

For quantity:

A pinch or speck	=	a scant ⅛ teaspoon, that is, one-half of ¼ teaspoon
3 teaspoons	=	1 tablespoon
4 tablespoons	=	¼ cup
8 tablespoons	=	½ cup
16 tablespoons	=	1 cup (8 fluid ounces)
2 cups	=	1 pint (fluid)
4 cups	=	1 quart (fluid)

Meat: The flesh of animals: beef from cattle, lamb from lambs, veal from calves and pork from hogs.

Meat—brand names: Given by packers or, sometimes,

wholesalers to established brands of processed, packaged and canned meat.

Meat—cleaning before cooking: Wipe with a cheesecloth
wrung out of cold water. Never leave meat in water;
soaking draws out meat juices.

Meat—color scheme: According to its color, meat is di-
vided into two groups: *red meat,* beef and lamb, may
be served rare, medium or well done; *white meat,*
pork and veal, must always be served well done.

Meat—composition: Any meat cut on the market has flesh
(called lean), fat and sometimes bones. Obviously,
some cuts have more lean, others more fat and/or
bone. The lean consists of muscle tissue which is held
together by connective tissue. The more a muscle has
been exercised, the more connective tissue is present
in the lean and the less tender is the meat, such as in
shoulder, flank, leg and breast cuts. The loin and rib
cuts have the most tender meat because muscles
along the animal's backbone are used the least.

The fat of meat is generally found on the outside of
a cut, and it can easily be trimmed. In some cuts,
small quantities of fat are distributed throughout the
lean; this marbling helps to make the meat more tender during cooking.

The bones, because of their distinct shapes, are the
best identifiers of a meat cut. Frequently, the name of
a meat cut is related to its bone structure; for instance, with an arm or blade roast or steak, shortribs, spareribs, breast of veal and lamb, neck bones,
back bones and riblets.

Meat juices: As referred to in this book, they are the
natural sauce or stock of pot roast, stews and braised
steaks, which are in the pot after cooking. Meat juices
may be served "as is" or thickened for gravy.

Meat–quality guides: Other than grading and stamping,
of which the average consumer sees very little, the
homemaker's best guides are a reliable meat market,

a reliable brand name and her own knowledge of meat cuts and how to cook them.

Meat—thermometer: To measure the accurate degree of doneness according to the internal temperature of meat; mainly used for roasts and thick steaks. In cooking pork, the use of a meat thermometer is strongly recommended.

　　To use: Insert in center of thickest part of meat. The bulb must not touch bone or fat.

Melt: To liquefy by heat. For meat, it usually means to liquefy fat.

Mince: To cut or chop into very small pieces, such as chives, mint or parsley.

Mix: To combine ingredients and blend thoroughly.

Oven temperatures: Measured in degrees Fahrenheit (° F):

very slow	250–275° F.
slow	300–325° F.
moderate	350–375° F.
hot	400–425° F.
very hot	450–475° F.

Pan-broil (grill): To cook, uncovered, on top of stove in a hot skillet or griddle either coated with fat or sprinkled with coarse salt before meat is placed in it. Fat is poured off as it accumulates during cooking.

Pan-fry: See *Sauté*.

Pork: The flesh of young hogs.

Preheat oven: Usually timed for 10 to 15 minutes before meat is put in to assure the desired temperature for cooking.

Rest the roast: To place meat on a hot platter or carving board to wait about 15 minutes before carving or slicing.

Roast: To cook by dry heat, uncovered, in the oven, in front of an open fire or on a spit.

Roaster: A covered or uncovered pan for oven-cooking, with or without a rack. Since it is often used for poultry, its size is designated by the weight of the bird it will hold.

Saucepan: A covered or uncovered cooking utensil with a handle; available in various sizes, with capacity stated in quarts. See *Skillet.*

Sauce pot: A cooking utensil larger than the saucepan, usually with two side handles; capacity is stated in quarts.

Sausage: Finely chopped meat or a combination of finely chopped meats blended with various seasonings; commonly stuffed into a casing or container.

Sauté: To brown or cook in a small amount of hot fat. See also: *Fry.*

Scallop: To bake, uncovered, usually cut-up foods with a sauce or other liquid; sometimes topped with grated cheese or buttered crumbs.

Seasonings: See *Spices, Herbs, Aromatic Seeds* and *Instant Seasonings.*

Skim: To remove fat from the surface of a hot liquid, usually by moving a flat spoon slowly across the surface.

Simmer: To cook a liquid or a food in liquid at temperatures of 185° F. to 210° F., just below the boiling point of water (212° F.). The liquid should be slightly agitated and form bubbles.

Skillet: A shallow fry pan with one handle and cover. Its size is stated by the top diameter in inches.

Spice blends: See *Spices.*

Spices: In the recipes of this book, all spices are ground, unless otherwise stated. The most commonly used spices in meat cookery are: allspice, cayenne (in moderation), cloves, ginger, mace, nutmeg, paprika, black pepper, white pepper, red pepper and saffron (in moderation). The spice blends are chili powder, curry powder, fines herbes, mixed pickling spices and poultry seasoning.

Steam: To cook in a steamer or pressure cooker by means of vapor from the boiling or simmering liquid.

Stew: To braise in a small amount of liquid; also referred to as "cubed meat."

Stir: To mix foods with a circular motion.

Stock: The water or liquid in which meat, fish, etc., has been cooked; usually referred to as beef stock, chicken stock, etc.; used as a base for soup and gravy. See *Bouillon.*

Thermometer: An instrument to measure temperature. See *Meat—Thermometer.*

Thicken: As referred to in this book, to make meat juices into a gravy with flour or cornstarch.

Timer: As referred to in this book, a small portable instrument which registers time, usually from 1 minute to 1 hour.

Toast: To brown in a toaster, broiler or oven or over hot coals.

Truss: To use string, skewers or toothpicks to keep meat in shape during cooking.

Variety meats: Sometimes called "specialty cuts" or "sundries," they include such organ meats as liver, brains, heart, kidney, sweetbreads, tongue and tripe. They are an excellent source of high-quality proteins, vitamins and minerals, with liver exceptionally rich in vitamin A.

Veal: The flesh of young calves (beef).

Whip: To beat food quickly and steadily, thereby increasing its volume and lightening its consistency. All utensils used to whip cream must be well chilled.

INDEX

(All cook-ahead dishes are marked with a *)

267